MANAGING FOR DEVELOPMENT

Managing for Development

Lifeskills International Ltd

Lifeskills team of writers:
Barrie Hopson
Jack Loughary
Steve Murgatroyd
Teresa Ripley
Mike Scally
Don Simpson

Lifeskills Series Editor: Jonathan Kitching

Gower

Published by
Gower Publishing Limited
Gower House
Croft Road
Aldershot
Hampshire GU11 3HR

Gower
Old Post Road
Brookfield
Vermont 05036
USA

British Library Cataloguing in Publication Data
Managing for development
1.Employees - Training of 2. Career development
I.Hopson, Barrie, 1943-
658.3 '124

ISBN 0 566 08140 7

Typeset in Middlesex by Setpoint and printed in Great Britain at the University Press, Cambridge.

Contents

Preface vii

1 People Development – It Comes with the Territory 1
Case in point 1
What is staff development? 5
Is staff development effective? 8
What is job satisfaction? 10
What can you do? 16
Observing 16
Informing 17
Coaching 17
Appraising 18
Counselling 20
Summary 21

2 Conducting a Development Review 23
Why organizations should commit to the personal and professional development of their people 23
The 70/30 rule – a philosophy for development 24
The nature of development 27
Typical blocks to self-development 28
Aspects of development 31
Learning styles and their significance for development 31
Competence-driven development 32
Summary 34
The value of development reviews 35
The difference between development reviews and performance reviews 36
The performance review 37
The development review 38
The development plan 40
Preparing for a development review 41
Interviewer's guide 42
How to get the most out of your development review 49
Development – a shared responsibility 49

Your role in development 51
Summary 56
Your development review 56
What can development do for the company? 57
Preparing for your development review and making the most of it 58
Summary 65

3 Manager as Coach 67
What is coaching? 67
The benefits of coaching 71
The obstacles to coaching 74
What does coaching give you? 76
Summary 77
The coaching process 78
The five stages of the coaching process 78
How adults learn 82
Learning styles 83
Factors that help or hinder learning 86
The learning curve 89
Rules of thumb 89
Recall time 90
Coaching skills 91
Summary 98
Making it work – applying and reviewing coaching skills 98
The coaching process in action 100
Summary – a final check 110

Index 113

Preface

Managing for Development includes a general introduction to this key function in organizational management and a treatment of three specific approaches: conducting staff development reviews, preparing staff for development reviews and staff coaching.

The purpose of Chapter 1 is to introduce managers to a view of the staff development territory that comes with management positions. It is an overview of the staff development function. The developmental review is offered in Chapter 2 as the foundation component of staff development for organizations. That foundation, in turn, is seen as a collaboration between a manager and staff members. The roles and responsibilities of both are discussed, along with suggested procedures for completing the process.

While managers play several roles in the delivery of staff development, coaching is viewed as one that is basic. It involves the interaction of managers and individual staff members aimed at assisting the staff members in understanding concepts and processes that are key to job performance. Coaching goes beyond organized instruction. Chapter 3 includes both general principles and coaching tips.

The book uses an open learning format in which readers are afforded a variety of opportunities to interact with the text material. The objectives of the open learning format are to offer readers a means of individualizing the material to relate it to their own experience and backgrounds and to their ongoing management responsibilities.

1

People Development – It Comes with the Territory

Case in point

A number of things come with your territory, depending on the particular area you have chosen or been assigned to manage. These might include bad weather, crowded motorways, poor train schedules, unfair competition and nights away from home. But one responsibility that comes with nearly every manager's territory is staff development. You may not run courses or deliver short-term training, but it is almost certain that some of your time as a manager will be devoted to helping your staff members grow in the job and develop their competencies.

'Nonsense!' some might respond. 'Why not just recruit the right person for the right job?'

What do you think? Why not just employ the right person for the job?

Your response may be worded differently, but the general idea is that jobs change and people change. Thus, even if you could find a person who met the job description perfectly, the specifications would probably have changed by the time you got around to engaging them. Furthermore, of course, the job description was never perfect in the first place. Secondly, that perfect person would probably change between the time you interviewed them and the time they reported for work. We live in a changing world, but job descriptions, frozen on paper, are more or less static.

Carrying out staff development can enhance your job satisfaction as a manager. Potential rewards for the activity include witnessing your staff improve, feeling good about solving problems and gaining respect from your staff, management colleagues and senior managers. More interestingly, perhaps, it can also enhance your potential for promotion within your organization and open up new opportunities outside. When senior managers are interviewed about the most rewarding and satisfying aspects of their management careers, they frequently put staff development high on the list.

In this chapter we will examine that part of the management territory called staff development and provide you with opportunities to clarify your thoughts about it.

Imagine that you are a manager arriving at work on Monday morning. Part of last week was spent interviewing shortlisted candidates for a vacancy in your team. You were pleased with the candidate finally selected and the people in personnel agreed with your choice.

You meet the smiling, eager new person, give them a brief orientation, introduce them to the supervisor responsible for their induction and wish them well. Four hours later you consult the supervisor and receive a very negative report. In short, you are told that a poor selection was probably made. You ask why, and learn that the new recruit lacks several skills specified in the job description that you believe are especially important. The new recruit claimed to have these skills during the interview but their performance appears to indicate otherwise.

To confirm the supervisor's observations, you spend most of the afternoon overseeing the new employee. Sure enough, by the end of the afternoon you too are convinced that a critical skill deficiency exists. Perhaps the new employee simply misunderstood the level of competency needed. Whatever the reason for the discrepancy, the person just cannot perform the functions involved in the position.

What should you do? Read the text below, circle the numbers of the options you might follow and rule out those you think are not feasible. Note your reasoning after each item.

1 Send the person packing and ask personnel for someone who meets the job specifications.

____

____

2 Reorganize staff work assignments to cover the problem.

____

____

3 Try to bring the new person up to speed as soon as possible.

____

____

4 Make do as best you can, hoping that time will sort it out: the person will learn or become discouraged and resign.

____

____

5 Help the person find a more suitable job.

____

____

6 Refer the person for career counselling.

____

____

Even though all of the options might be suitable in some situations, some are not appropriate in this situation. Below is our reasoning. Compare the following with your thinking.

1 If the person is seriously mismatched with the position (for example, lacks the technical skills required), this may be an appropriate response. Why make everyone miserable and penalize the rest of the department for production problems? (Be tactful with the individual and with the personnel department, of course, if you want its future cooperation.) If the mismatch is not that serious, then perhaps you should continue looking at other alternatives. After all, isn't a manager expected to be a problem solver?

2 Given a sufficient number of staff, this would be a feasible solution. However, in this situation you have a relatively small staff and the person who has the required competency fills a key position, so this is not an option.

3 Bringing a person up to speed implies changing their behaviour. How serious is the discrepancy between the job requirements and the person's ability level? Will simply providing more information suffice? This would be fine if you have the information and time to present it, or have someone else who does. Or is it a matter of the employee learning a routine or skill? If so, mentoring might do the trick. Can you or someone else provide some on-the-job, hands-on, 'show and tell' time with the person while they learn what is needed? Is there enough time to find out exactly what is causing the problem? For example, learning a skill on a wordprocessor can be a short task, while learning to deal with angry customers may take a great deal of time and practice.

4 Making do and leaving to happenstance doesn't have a ring of wisdom to it, even though it is often seen as a solution. This will not do except as a very temporary remedy – unless, of course, the discrepancy is minor and is likely to correct itself shortly. In this instance it is not.

5 and 6 Assisting the person in finding another job or career counselling may be appropriate longer-term staff-development strategies in the right context. In some organi-

> zations, for example, managers meet regularly with staff members to discuss problems and more general career concerns. If job dissatisfactions come up in such a discussion, career counselling or a job change might be appropriate, but in the illustrative situation neither is appropriate. As a manager, your immediate problem is in reducing the discrepancy between job requirements and a newly recruited person who does not meet them.

To return to the point, it is only Monday and you are already doing staff development!

What is staff development?

Staff development could be described as any effort to support employees in increasing their competencies and growing in their jobs. Practically speaking, organizations will probably define staff development along a continuum of possible employee-assistance activities. At one end of the continuum are clearly job-related interventions. Examples of these direct and specific interventions are job coaching, on-the-job remedial training and job reassignment. The other end of the staff-development continuum could stretch all the way to organizing courses and providing paid sabbatical leave. That an increasing number of employers offer such staff development opportunities is indeed progress, and some unions have negotiated for sabbatical leave options to be written into their members' contracts.

Between these two ends of the staff-development continuum are other kinds of provision. Examples are job and career counselling, treatment for drug and alcohol abuse, reimbursement of tuition fees for external courses, in-house courses both during and outside working hours (both job related and non-job related), childcare, job training for spouses and reimbursement of travel costs in support of some of these.

How aware are you of staff-development opportunities provided by your organization? List some of which you are aware overleaf. What is your general opinion regarding these?

Staff development ranges from the remedial to the purely developmental. The example just discussed involves an instance of staff development initiated by a manager. The manager was motivated to solve an organizational problem; that is, an employee assigned to a job for which he or she lacked the specified competencies or qualifications. Other motivations to initiate staff development include requests from individual employees, informal groups of employees, organized groups such as departments, other managers, corporate staff and sources outside the organization, such as governmental and professional groups.

Remedial, or corrective, staff development is usually based on an observation by someone at management level. In many cases the observation is that something is not as it should be, such as an employee not performing as expected, a group not producing as projected, some quality shortfalls in products or services or an unacceptably high incidence of absenteeism or accidents. The observation may be in real time, such as a manager becoming aware of an individual's poor performance, or it may be historical, such as a manager studying past costs and production reports. Incidentally, computerized monitoring of an increasing variety of processes has reduced the time lag between incidents of poor performance and an awareness that these require a response. This often allows remedial staff development to take place much nearer the situation that is making the need apparent.

Preventive staff development is similar to remedial in that it is done in response to a potential problem. The problem has not yet emerged, but there is good reason to predict that it will, at least enough to warrant developmental intervention. Closely related may be a staff development effort carried out to ensure compliance with a government policy of some kind. Interestingly, development to support compliance when initiated without adequate employee support or sympathy can itself be a source of morale problems for managers, which in turn calls for additional staff development.

What might be labelled pure, 'values-driven' staff development is done in the absence of even potential problems. It is often a case of higher-level management believing, presuming or hoping that organizational benefit will result from investment in staff development. The benefit could be as general as feeling good about contributing to employee development, rewarding high achievement or service, public goodwill or some serendipitous benefit. More often than not, management holds the philosophical belief that good does come from most human development.

A related reason for manager-initiated staff development might be called, for lack of a more accurate term, intuition. Stemming from whatever cause, a manager may have a hunch that initiating a programme, or providing a particular benefit to staff, would be motivational or inspirational, which in turn might have a positive and more tangible outcome. For example, you may recall the free bran muffin programme initiated when your manager read that eating a cup of bran a day would make employees more alert and thus might reduce accident rates!

What kinds of staff development have you participated in or observed? Note examples and the roles you played in them. What were the outcomes of the examples?

Remedial (or corrective):

____

____

Preventive:

____

____

Values driven:

Intuitive:

If you can, identify an example of a particularly interesting staff-development effort and note why it happened and what resulted.

What is your reflection on the inferences you can draw from this discussion regarding staff development as a management tool for you?

Is staff development effective?

It is probably true that the grander the staff-development scheme, the less specific are the stated desired outcomes. Many years ago in the US, Henry Ford raised every employee's wages in his company and provided other kinds of benefit. He expected as a result to make lots of money; and he did. Other companies followed his lead and went bankrupt. Ford probably knew precisely how employees would change their behaviour at work, and thus plant production, as a result of improving benefits. However, because he was president of the corporation, no one forced him to write it down.

Ultimately, employers expect staff development to increase production, generate higher profits, improve labour relations, decrease employee turnover and reduce training costs. Whether or not such objectives are met by staff development is difficult to answer because so many other conditions are involved. For example, do your staff produce more because of what they learned from a course they requested and you arranged? Or is their changed work behaviour a result of their greater regard for you in response to your concern for their professional development (and perhaps a change in routine)? Or perhaps it is partly due to good morale resulting from the company sports team winning its league competition during the same week as the training. Or is it all three? It is difficult to say. Wouldn't it be nice if personnel research were as easy as testing one brand of detergent against another?

Research suggests that we are more likely to get a useful answer to the question of outcomes from staff development if the expected outcomes are carefully stated. It is even better if the question is employer specific. For example, increasing wages seems to improve production in some companies, but not in others. Giving workers a voice in developing policy may boost worker morale in one organization but have no effect in another, or it may make a difference with younger employees but not older ones. In part, it is how the question is asked and what is used to measure change that enables you to evaluate staff-development efforts.

If there is a general principle to follow, it is to make your connection between management expectations and staff-development efforts as clear as possible. In other words, develop a clear idea of what you expect from a staff-development process. Also check your assumptions.

For example, it is often stated that 'happy employees are productive employees'. What do you think? Are they?

Note an example or two from your experience to support that statement and another to refute it.

The data is not all in, and may never be, but one would be wise not to accept the 'happy worker' claim at face value. While some happy workers exceed production norms, there are many groups of happy workers whose production is inadequate. The important point for managers is to be as certain as you can that the objectives of your staff-development efforts are likely to achieve your goals. There may be positive outcomes from a staff-development programme, such as high morale and good worker/manager rapport. However, is that important if your goal of an increase in production is not met? There is nothing wrong with creating happy workers, of course, but is that a sufficient outcome of staff-development efforts? Put another way, there are many factors that affect production and many that affect worker morale, and they are not all the same factors.

What is job satisfaction?

Worker performance is a function of motivation. While money, or what it will purchase, remains a significant motivator for most workers, it is no longer the most important reason for selling one's time and effort to an employer. When your standard of living reaches a certain level and you are reasonably sure that it will continue, other types of motivators increase in importance and, as we implied earlier, different things motivate different people.

Managers are continually having to confront the issue of differing motivations within a group of staff. Some workers prefer more income and others more discretionary time, for example. Sometimes both can have what they want; at other times, a compromise may be the answer.

The next exercise is designed to explore the implications for managers. It deals with the concept of different job 'pay-offs'.

The term 'pay-off' is a straightforward way of recognizing that people choose between different kinds of activity depending on the pay-offs that each can provide. (This material on job pay-offs was developed based on research by Herzberg.) Your pay-off (anticipated pleasure) for attending the cinema may be greater than that for playing a round of golf. Assuming you can afford both, the preferred pay-off motivates you to do one over the other. The same concept applies to work, assuming that you have a choice of jobs, each with its own set of pay-offs.

In this example, assume that you are being interviewed for a job at Ajax box factory. After discussing your qualifications and having assured himself that you are a moral being, Mr Ajax finally gets around to reimbursement.

He says, 'I want you to come to my box factory and work eight hours a day. You will work in a ten-person box-assembly group. I keep the group room clean, well lit and adequately ventilated. The group is allowed to organize itself as to the division of labour, rest periods and so forth. In general, I expect you to make one box per hour. You will earn £8 for each eight-hour day. If you fall behind a little in your output, that is OK and your group will help you catch up. But remember, you may be expected to do the same for some other slow coach. But the deal is that at the end of the week you will have worked five eight-hour days and made a total of 40 boxes, for which I will pay you £40.'

'Or I have another deal that you may like better,' Mr Ajax continues. 'You come to my factory every day and make eight boxes and I will pay you £1 a box. You may work whatever hours you want as long as you give me eight boxes at the end of each day. You will work by yourself in a dirty, dimly lit, unheated back room. This is also where I store supplies and people may forget to shut the door as they come and go. At the end of each day when you deliver the eight boxes you built, I will pay you £8. In both deals you make £40 and I get 40 boxes per week. Which do you want?'

Which of Mr Ajax's deals would you take? Deal 1 or Deal 2?

____

____

Explain the reasons for your selection.

'But just a moment,' Ajax says as you are about to close the deal. 'I have a third deal that might interest you. It is this. You come to the factory every Monday morning and I will provide you with enough lumber and screws to make 40 boxes. I will also show you how I make them. You take away the materials and at the end of five days deliver to me 40 finished boxes just like the ones I make in the factory. I will pay you £1 each, or £40 for the 40 boxes. Now which deal do you prefer?'

Would you change your mind? Which deal to you prefer – Deal 1, Deal 2 or Deal 3?

Briefly explain your reasons for changing your mind or sticking with your original choice.

As you know, there is no correct answer and, of course, the choices are never that simple in real life. Yet we do usually have an option that we prefer and sometimes it seems strange that everyone doesn't agree with our preferences. Different strokes for different folks. In the next section we examine more systematically the issue of job pay-offs.

There is a good chance that you revealed something about your preferences for job pay-offs in the last exercise. As we noted, these refer to some feature or condition that you prefer and anticipate getting in exchange for performing a job. You also know that people have different job pay-off preferences. However, the potential pay-offs can be summarized in surprisingly few categories – about 10, to be precise.

The 10 kinds of pay-off are:

1 achievement
2 recognition for achievement
3 doing the work itself
4 responsibility associated with the work
5 opportunity for advancement
6 policy and administration of the employer
7 nature of the supervision
8 salary
9 interpersonal relationships
10 working conditions.

What follows is a quick reckoning of the three deals you were offered by Ajax in terms of job pay-offs.

1 *Achievement.* Achievement was clear in each deal, namely the knowledge that you completed 40 boxes a week. In all three deals the completed boxes would be clear measures of your achievement.
2 *Recognition for achievement.* People who place a high value on receiving recognition for achievement would probably prefer Deal 2 over Deal 1 because, with Deal 2, the recognition comes at the end of each day when the product is turned over to Mr Ajax. This recognition of achievement comes only once a week in Deal 1. But don't overlook the potential recognition for achievement in Deal 3. If you handle it right, get more work and keep costs down, you could make a lot of money over time. That's added recognition for achievement!
3 *The work itself.* At first glance, the work seems very similar in each situation; making a wooden box is making a wooden box. However, in Deal 1 you have your say in deciding how the work is being divided so you might do more sawing than nailing so, if sawing turns you on, you might prefer Deal 1.

Deal 2 does not offer that option. The fun starts with Deal 3. For example, if you actually dislike both nailing and sawing, Deal 3 may be your cup of tea because there is the implicit opportunity to be an entrepreneur. You could start your own company and even subcontract the work to some people who will work for less than you do, allowing you to realize a profit. Deal 3 may allow you to achieve the kind of job pay-offs you really enjoy, in the form of 'wheeling and dealing'.

4 *Responsibility associated with the work.* Deals 1 and 2 are low in this regard. Mr Ajax retains control over the process. He takes care of the supplies and hands out the tools. Deal 3, of course, is full of work responsibility because, after getting the material, the show is all yours, whether you do it alone, with others or subcontract it.

5 *Potential for advancement.* As described, Deals 1 and 2 are very poor regarding potential for climbing the vocational ladder. Deal 1 may score somewhat higher against this pay-off because the group work may provide an opportunity to show off your administrative and creative abilities, as well as your marvellous interpersonal skills, all of which would put your name on the shortlist for Mr Ajax's next assistant to the assistant manager position. Potential for advancement does not apply to Deal 3 because, if you take it, you remove yourself from the Ajax organization.

6 *Policy and administration of the organization.* This pay-off refers to the impact that the employer's policy and administrative procedures have on employees. It does not seem to be important in any of the three deals. Ajax probably hires workers on a casual basis and, other than that, is without policy or administrative procedures that would make any pay-off differences to you. However, if Mr Ajax changes his style and starts giving employment preference to people who live within walking distance of the factory, are married without children and are over six feet tall, then you might pay more attention to this pay-off. At least you would compare it to that of Wooden Box Works down the street. In Deal 3 you essentially make your own policy, and that may be appealing.

7 *Supervision.* There is an important difference regarding supervision between Deals 1 and 2. If you prefer to work without supervision, then Deal 2 is definitely for you. In Deal 3, supervision is a moot point unless, of course, you are talking about yourself doing the supervising!
8 *Salary.* Deals 1 and 2 pay the same. You might make a fortune in Deal 3, but that is not really a salary. The reimbursement arrangement in Deal 3 should be considered under the pay-off 'recognition for achievement'. It is, specifically, the potential for profit. Then don't forget Wooden Box Works. Salary as a pay-off is limited at Ajax, but if you look further into the industry and broaden your horizons, a higher salary could be a sufficient pay-off for considering a move to Wooden.
9 *Interpersonal relationships.* This one is obvious. Whether you are gregarious or reclusive, there is a clear choice – if the former you will prefer Deal 1; if the latter, Deal 2 is for you. Don't forget also that there is potential for both positive and negative interpersonal relationships in Deal 3. It will be more difficult to predict. In addition, as you well know, interpersonal relationships can always be highly influenced by the final pay-off, the working conditions.
10 *Working conditions.* The choice between Deals 1 and 2 is clear. In this example, the 'working conditions' pay-off serves to illustrate the trade-offs that may be involved in obtaining the mix of pay-offs that is most appealing. For example, for some people cleanliness of the work site is so strong as to override any other pay-off, whereas others can't bear to work alone.

That illustrates one final point. The pay-off potential is seldom a simple either/or situation. The decision for most workers involves weighing and comparing multiple pay-offs. The more pay-offs are involved, the more difficult is the decision. Managers can make an important contribution to staff development by helping to make the pay-off situation clear to employees. Managers are more likely to perceive the larger picture than are less experienced staff members.

What can you do?

There are many ways to assist individual staff members in developing information, skills, competencies and even attitudes. We have mentioned some of these already. This section contains more systematic descriptions and illustrations of several more or less 'standard' techniques for helping employees develop. One hesitates to use the word 'techniques', because each is probably as much an art as a skill. Nevertheless, it will be useful to be aware of alternative ways of helping and to have a language for talking about them.

Observing

Probably the most effective way to recognize an individual's development needs is to observe the person in a problem situation. Most problems are likely to be a product of the interaction between an individual and the setting. This may not be as simple to do as it appears. The difficulty of making valid observations has landed more than one manager in trouble.

An important aspect of valid observations is knowing what it is you are looking for. For example, it is not unusual for observers to be preoccupied with what an employee is doing wrong. In practice, you are often more likely to understand the problem if you try to discover what they are doing right. The reason is that most people want to perform a job well. Few really want to make errors. That being true, most people think that they are performing well most of the time and are upset when they do not produce the desired results. The wise manager will try to observe the mistakes in assumptions, understandings and judgement that underlie the inappropriate or ineffective behaviour.

In addition, strive to observe what the person is doing from their own perspective, not only from yours. Don't confuse their view with yours; you are both unique and different. Psychologists point out that sloppy and careless observations can tell us much more about the observer than the observed. If you can get into an employee's shoes and see a situation from their frame of reference, then you are more likely to understand their behaviour.

For example, as a manager, you may think that a cashier's failure to give the correct change is due to deficient skills of arithmetic. Therefore, you concentrate on helping her improve her ability to add and subtract. Actually, if you had observed more carefully, you would have seen that the cashier is so preoccupied with preventing you from discovering that she doesn't understand one or two operations of the cash register that she often makes errors giving change, especially when you are standing near her. Check your assumptions by trying to consider how the ineffective performer might perceive the situation.

Informing

Employees are often inadequately informed about their assignments. Their understanding of what is expected of them is incomplete or inaccurate.

For example, you gave detailed instructions to the new cashier. You thought you had covered everything important and you probably had. Remember, however, that while you assumed that she was paying full attention to you she was also trying to remember which locker was hers, the uniform schedule for the week, the options about lunch and tea breaks and the name of her immediate supervisor. She's very likely to have missed something! During your instruction, she probably focused on things that seemed most immediate to her. What may seem like a large problem may simply be a matter of repeating instructions when she can pay closer attention and is ready to take the information on board.

One rule of thumb is to assume that people will only remember part of what you tell them. This is not necessarily their fault; it is just the way things are. So save yourself and them a great deal of trouble and find out what they remember, then repeat what they missed. Make sure that a development session doesn't produce an information overload. People may not need as much information as you think they do. Find out what they need.

Coaching

Coaching employees involves working alongside or close to them, helping when help is most needed. If you have been part of an athletics team or taken individual music, art or other kinds of one-to-one lessons, you have probably experienced being coached. It is a form of individualized instruction. A key point is that in a coaching situation the learner (employee) and the coach (manager) participate in setting learning goals. In coaching, attention should be on what the learner wants to learn, not on a schedule of learning tasks.

A good assumption to make is that coaching will take more than one interaction. Part of successful coaching is the coach and the learner getting to know one another well enough to be open without the fear of offending the other. Most successful coaching probably appears to be spontaneous. It may be, but it can also be systematic in that you, as coach, are immediately responsive to an opportunity to help and you build on an established coaching relationship. Effective coaching is usually precise, purposeful and supportive. If you think about it, it's difficult to be totally spontaneous in achieving that!

Appraising

Appraising an employee is a combination of measurement, evaluation and communication. The three components can be confused, resulting in an ineffective intervention.

- Measurement is concerned with how much – it is quantitative.
- Evaluation is concerned with how good – it is qualitative.
- Communication is concerned with informing – it is enlightening.

Imagine that you manage a group of 20 assistants in a department store. Every six months one of your tasks is to appraise them of how well they are performing their jobs. Let's say that you need to focus on three levels of measurement: 'below average', 'average' and 'above average'. After observing the assistants' work, you assign each of them one of the three measures.

Now pretend that you are one of the assistants and you have been told that you measure 'below average'. What might that mean to you?

Would you expect to lose your job? Explain your answer.

Many people would expect to lose their job. Suppose you were told, 'True you are below average as compared with this particular group of assistants, but the group as a whole is made up of highly exceptional assistants'. How might that affect your interpretation of 'below average'?

So compared to the elite group of 20 assistants, of which you are one, you are below average. But compared to assistants in general, you are a whiz! And the job remains yours! The point is that when you are measuring a person's performance you should have a reference point.

The same is true of evaluation. This takes place after you have made a measurement. It asks the question, 'Is this measurement good enough for job *x*?'. If, for example, you were assembling a group of computer technicians to work on a very important project, then technicians who came out with an 'average' rating from their supervisors probably would not be 'good enough' for your group.

When it comes to communicating your evaluation to staff members, it is important that they understand the measure you used, how it was obtained and the criteria you used to arrive at the judgement. Appraisal, as you see, can become complex. This is why it is best to use numbers when measuring, to be explicit about norm or reference groups when evaluating and to try to talk on a one-to-one basis when you are communicating.

Counselling

Counselling is done by people representing a wide and varied range of professional training and experience. Unfortunately, not every kind is expert. Counselling can serve many purposes. Three examples are cathartic listening, personal or career decisions and psychotherapy.

In the context of staff development, most professional counsellors would probably agree that counselling done by managers should be limited to specific job-related issues and preliminary career concerns. The reasoning behind this recommendation is that when people are emotionally upset it is often helpful to talk with an objective, trusted person who is not offering advice. An experienced manager may or may not meet those criteria. An objective, empathetic listener can enhance the employee's potential for making effective decisions about the next steps to take in resolving their problems. In addition to active listening, counselling in these kinds of situation might also include providing information regarding other sources of help or support.

The rationale for managers undertaking initial career counselling is that employees may see the manager as a logical starting point. Some, of course, may have the opposite perception, but a respected and trusted manager may be instrumental in helping an employee sort out their job and career problems and decide on an initial plan for development and eventual change.

Reflect on the ways discussed in this section in which managers contribute to the development of their people.

Which of them have your managers used to help you with your development and were they effective?

Which are you aware of using in your management of others and which have you found most effective?

In your organization, how much is it accepted that it is a part of a manager's role to develop people?

What are the qualities and skills that you feel are most evident in those managers who are most effective at staff development?

What would you say are your current strengths as a 'people developer' and what would you like to be better at?

Summary

Staff development is an important and professionally rewarding aspect of managing people. Its specific functions and activities vary with the level of management and the nature of the organization. Effective staff development requires a knowledge of job pay-offs and how employees respond to these. This is because most occupational behaviour is based on worker motivation, which nearly always involves a combination of job pay-off expectations.

If staff-development programmes are to be effective, managers need to understand their possible implications as well as expected outcomes. Staff-development efforts can result in happy workers with or without having an impact on production. There are many approaches to staff development. Observation of staff and a clear purpose is an important basis for all staff development.

2

Conducting a Development Review

Why organizations should commit to the personal and professional development of their people

As we look around us at business today, what do we see?

- Increased competition.
- Greater emphasis on quality.
- The need to get products and services ever more quickly to the marketplace.
- Volatility in customer demands and requirements.
- Customers demanding ever greater customization of general products and services.

To satisfy those requirements, businesses need a highly flexible, committed workforce, able to respond quickly to rapid change, able to develop new skills and continually acquire new know-how. If their people lack these qualities, companies will find it increasingly difficult to remain competitive. Education, training and staff development are crucial to providing this flexibility and adaptability in the workforce, as is your contribution as a manager and developer of the people who work for you.

Many existing employees will have left school many years ago and a significant number will not have received any formal education or training since then. For these people especially, a great deal of help and encouragement will be required if they are to return to learning and see it as being intrinsically fulfilling as well as an economic necessity for the company.

The 70/30 rule – a philosophy for development

There is a growing body of evidence to support the conclusion that people development is vital to business success. However, not just any development programme will do. Here are some guiding principles that we believe are essential for any well-designed people-development provision:

- The company must have a very clear philosophy about development and this must be communicated to everybody in the business.
- It is unhealthy for individuals to believe that their development is the company's responsibility or for the company to believe that it is all the responsibility of the individual. Development needs to be a two-way contract, a shared responsibility.
- A clear development philosophy should be based on business needs and individual motivation; that is, it should be mutually beneficial.

We believe in the 70/30 rule for development. In this, a company states that it believes strongly in people development and, at the same time, believes that it is better for people to be self-managing and to take charge of their own development. The message from the company is:

70 per cent of the responsibility for your development belongs to you and 30 per cent of it belongs to the company. To fulfil our 30 per cent, the company will:

- *keep you informed of future business plans and needs*
- *provide you with opportunities to reflect on your own learning and career-development needs*
- *operate an effective performance-management scheme that will give you accurate feedback on your performance against corporate plans*
- *provide learning opportunities for you to develop your career in the light of company plans and your own aspirations.*

At the same time as we provide opportunities for you to develop yourself, we will expect you to take responsibility for your own development.

Does your organization follow the 70/30 rule? If not, what is its development philosophy?

Are you kept informed of future business plans and needs?

Are there opportunities to reflect on your own learning and career development needs? If so, how?

Is there an effective performance-management scheme that gives people accurate feedback on their performance against corporate plans?

Are there learning opportunities for you to develop your career in the light of company plans and your own aspirations? If so, what are they?

Think about those you manage. Do you give them opportunities to reflect on their own learning and career-development needs?

Do you give them regular and accurate feedback on their performance against plans?

What opportunities do you give them to develop themselves and their careers?

This chapter will help you to understand and develop the 70/30 rule in your organization. It looks at:

- the nature of development
- the logistics of development – what the organization's responsibility is and what the individual's role is
- the value of a personal and professional development review to the organization and to you and the people you manage
- the structure and content of a review
- the difference between development reviews and performance reviews
- the output of a review – a personal and professional development plan
- a generic structure for a review form.

Reading the chapter before you begin to use development reviews will help clarify your objectives and ensure that the experience is valuable for both you and those you manage.

The nature of development

Learning is the new form of labour. It is no longer a separate activity that occurs either before one enters the workplace or in remote classroom settings ... Learning is the heart of productive activity.

Shoshana Zuboff, In the Age of the Smart Machine

Before you explore the details, it is worth taking a step back to think more deeply about what development involves. This section therefore looks at the nature of development and the different environments in which it can be achieved. You will be asked to look at your own development and the barriers and obstacles that you have encountered. This will give you an insight into the barriers and obstacles that your staff will face. Then you will look at the key role of the development review in helping your team develop both professionally and personally.

Personal and professional development is about continually improving what we do and how we do it. To develop we need to learn. Sometimes we will need to learn new skills; at other times it will be new knowledge; sometimes we will want to develop whole new ways of looking at the world and, as a consequence, our attitudes, opinions, beliefs and even our values may change. Learning is an everyday, ongoing experience. The process begins within minutes of birth (and, some would argue, even before that). It is not something that happens only in a classroom.

All too many people have been put off learning by the rigid frameworks imposed by educational systems. The job of people developers is often to rekindle the flame of learning that never quite leaves us. It is the ability to learn and adapt continuously that makes human beings a successful species.

People develop in many different ways in their everyday lives – by watching, listening, asking questions, trying things out, researching, experimenting, practising, reading, watching television, listening to tapes, carrying out projects, solving problems, making decisions, challenging conflicts and going on courses. Part of what you can offer your team is the opportunity to continue that development while they are at work.

Development is not just another word for training. It is much broader, as we have seen. Development encompasses training but, unlike training, it does not have a beginning and an end. It goes on long after the individual's training course ends. Somebody made the distinction, 'Training is for this job, development is for this and your future ones!'.

Development is about personal growth and, as such, the determination to develop must, ideally, come from within each person. What an organization can do is provide the tools and climate for learning that will encourage and empower people to embark on and take charge of their own development.

Development is as much a way of travelling as a precise destination … the destination will be determined to a great extent by the way one travels.

Bernard Ouedraogo

How is your own journey going? Before you go on to review your staff's development, take a look at your own development. It will give you valuable material to draw on. What are some of the barriers and obstacles that you face in your own journey of self-development? They could be to do with your own feelings, the organization's culture or your domestic situation.

Typical blocks to self-development

Some frequently heard statements are listed below. Are any of them familiar to you?

- I won't be given time off to do it.
- I was never very good at school.
- I'm not very good at learning.
- I won't be able to get the job I really want, so what's the point of learning new things?
- It's not my job to work out what I need to learn. You tell me what I need to know.
- I don't know what I'm really interested in doing.
- I don't know what I want to do next in my career.
- I don't know enough about what's important to me.

- I've never thought much about the future.
- What's the point? When I've done things like this before no one has given me any recognition for it.
- I'm too busy.

These are all familiar refrains, some of which you have probably heard from members of your staff. Which have you said yourself? Which have you heard others use as reasons for not engaging in learning? Now look at the responses below to these self-made barriers to development.

It will be useful to bear the list of barriers in mind as you commit to developing your people. They are 'stoppers' that need to be challenged.

Blocking statement: I won't be given any time off to do it.
Response: The 70/30 rule means that both you and the organization have a shared responsibility. You will be given some time to do this, but you will also have to find time yourself.

Blocking statement: I was never very good at school.
Blocking statement: I'm not very good at learning.
Response: Development is not about school-type learning. As an adult, you will learn differently, through activity, through experience. You will also be given help to get started.

Blocking statement: I won't be able to get the job I really want, so what's the point of learning new things?
Response: First, you can never be certain what job you will or will not get and, secondly, learning new things will reveal other possibilities for you that, as yet, you may not even have thought of. Also, learning can be fun in itself and can open up new interests. This will be satisfying to you if by some chance you don't make the career move that you want or as soon as you want. Security in the future will come from being multi-skilled and always having alternatives. Continuous development will be the route to that.

Blocking statement: It's not my job to work out what I need to learn. You tell me what I need to know.
Response: What happens to you is more to do with you than with the organization. We will help you to develop in ways that we need, but what about the ways in which you want to develop? We also want people who are prepared to take greater charge of their own learning, because our future success depends on team members who are self-directing, flexible and who can think for themselves. People who are dependent and reactive will gain less and be significantly less attractive to employers than responsibility-taking, proactive individuals.

Blocking statement: I don't know what I'm really interested in doing.
Blocking statement: I don't know what I want to do next in my career.
Blocking statement: I don't know enough about what's important to me.
Blocking statement: I've never thought much about the future.
Response: Development reviews and further training will help you think through the things that you are good at and not so good at, as well as help you work out what you're interested in and what is important to you about work and the rest of your life too. It is a very valuable investment of time periodically to take stock of how you feel about your career and your life.

Blocking statement: What's the point? When I've done things like this before, no one has given me any recognition for it.
Response: The difference is that this system is planned and agreed by both you and your manager. You will keep in touch with your manager, reviewing and discussing your progress as you go and adapting it where necessary. Also, the reason why a company introduces a development review system is actively to encourage people to take greater charge of their own development. People who use this opportunity will have an excellent chance of a better future.

Blocking statement: I'm too busy.
Response: Personal and professional development is a key priority for business success and, as such, we cannot emphasize enough the importance of making time for this activity. The company is putting time, money and resources into your development. As that is a shared responsibility and as it is your own development, it is important that you do too.

Are there any other negative statements you can think of – and answer – that might arise?

Aspects of development

Learning styles and their significance for development

Just as there are different personality styles, so there are different styles of learning. Some people learn best by experimenting and doing, others by reflecting and thinking. Some people learn best in the company of others while some learn best alone. Some learn by listening while others learn by watching or feeling.

Most people have a good idea of their preferred way of learning even if they do not understand why one style suits them better than another. Any development strategy needs to take these different styles into account and should ensure that there is a wide variety of learning opportunities and media for learning. Not everyone enjoys face-to-face learning. Some people prefer open learning (as in the format of this book), others prefer learning on a computer or interactive video, others like reading while still others prefer audio tapes. Some people like specific instruction while others like to discover things for themselves.

How well do the learning opportunities available in your organization cater for all of these differences? Do you have an effective, flexible learning-delivery strategy?

Competence-driven development

Increasingly, companies are analysing the criteria that separate superior performance from average performance. On an individual level, these characteristics or criteria are called competences. Competence can be defined as 'the ability of the individual to perform to the standards required in particular jobs'. Competences state what individuals should be able to do if they are doing their jobs competently.

Competences differ in the extent to which they can be taught or developed. Knowledge and skills are the easiest to teach; changing attitudes and values is much harder; and changing motives or basic personality style is lengthy, difficult and expensive. Indeed, in some cases it may be impossible.

Some companies have designed competence-driven recruitment and selection programmes that they feed into their development programmes.

Do you recruit for motivation and personality style and develop knowledge and skills later?

Do you analyse jobs before recruiting in order to identify key qualities and competence profiles of successful performers?

Do employees understand exactly what competences are required to succeed in a given job?

Do you use competence profiles as the basis for individual development programmes?

Do employees understand what competences they will need to develop and move into a different job?

'Yes' responses to these questions suggest that your company is already quite a way along the path towards developing an integrated and well-coordinated recruitment, selection and development strategy.

If you have answered 'No' to any question, make some notes about how you might help turn your 'No' into a 'Yes'.

The general advice is to recruit for motives and personality style and develop knowledge and skills later. Unfortunately, many organizations do the opposite – they hire people on the basis of their educational credentials and hope that the recruits can be persuaded into thinking and behaving appropriately. Ted

Fowler, the president of US restaurant chain Golden Corrall, has a sign on his wall that says simply:

Never try to teach a pig to sing … it wastes your time and annoys the pig.

Ideally, a company's key jobs will have been analysed by identifying the characteristics of the best performers in those jobs and then defining competence profiles for each of the jobs. One benefit of this is that the mystery is immediately taken out of internal recruitment and succession. An employee can be shown exactly what it will take to be successful in any particular job. If she wants to aim for that position, she and her managers will know precisely the competences she should be developing before she applies for that position.

If competence profiles have been developed for a number of jobs in the company, they are a valuable addition to personal and professional development programmes. Both manager and employee can examine these profiles together and develop an action plan to aid the employee's further development.

Many leading companies – for example, Boots, ICI, Mobil and BP – already have a large number of competence profiles that form the basis of their development programmes.

Summary

In this section we have looked at the nature of development. You have reflected on your company's approach to development and considered some of the obstacles that may impede development for yourself and your team. You have also looked at the learning opportunities available in your company and considered whether or not there is a clear and coordinated recruitment, selection and development strategy based on competences.

The next section will focus on development reviews and development plans, as the core of a coordinated approach. These can be used to prompt future-oriented development action.

The value of development reviews

We have already indicated that those companies that invest in developing their people claim substantial economic benefits. But if a company does make the decision to do this, where does it start? In a business setting, learning is best encouraged and managed by introducing development reviews and their associated outputs, development plans.

What can development reviews provide for you and the people you manage? Many of us live from day to day. We have jobs, we may feel we have careers, and we have lives outside of work. We are so involved in the 'dailyness' of our everyday life that we rarely take the time to pause and think about whether it is really satisfying, or what we might do to make it more satisfying. We all know that it is vital to stop occasionally to review and reflect. Perhaps the most valuable benefit of a development review is that it provides an opportunity for the people you manage to gain an overview of their lives.

More specifically, it is a chance for them to:

- think about their future
- collect data about themselves – their skills, interests, the type of people they are, what is important and unimportant to them about work and their preferred career pattern
- find out what future opportunities there might be for them in the company
- think about how they like to learn and what resources are available to them to help them learn and develop
- discuss their development needs openly with you
- make suggestions as to how you and the company could help them develop
- produce a personal and professional development plan.

It is not:

- an opportunity to discuss particular work issues or problems in their present job
- about salary issues.

What can a development review system provide for the company? It is a chance for an open exchange of views and information between you and those you manage. In particular, it is an opportunity for you to find out more about what they want from the company and see if they can design a plan together with a manager to help them achieve it.

A company that implements a development review system achieves the following overall benefits:

- It has a clearer idea of what it can do to help people to develop, which will assist in cultivating a more flexible and adaptable workforce. This is vital to business success, as it is people who provide a key differentiation between a company and its competition.
- It is less likely to offer people inappropriate career opportunities.
- It can give people realistic information about career and professional development prospects.
- Through feedback, it may identify internal needs of which it is currently unaware.

The difference between development reviews and performance reviews

Many successful organizations are now beginning to differentiate between a performance review and a development review. However, others continue to combine the two in a single event, which can lead to difficulties.

Does your organization give development or performance reviews? Tick the statements below that best describe your organization's reviews.

- They are linked directly to the business plan.
- They link individuals' objectives to overall business objectives.
- They focus on individuals' performance over a set period.
- They examine performance criteria from previous reviews and new performance criteria are agreed.

- They work through specific personal and professional development steps for the individual within the context of the organization's development strategy.
- They link the organization's development strategy to its business plan.

If you ticked all six of the above statements, then your reviews are about both development and performance. The first four statements are more to do with performance and the last two concern development.

Now read the descriptions below.

The performance review

A performance review is ideally linked directly to the business plan. It enables a manager to determine an employee's objectives to help achieve the business plan.

Typically, it takes the form of a session involving a manager and a member of staff in which the focus of the session is primarily on the staff member's present job and how he or she has been performing in it. Performance criteria from the previous review are examined and new performance criteria are defined and agreed. The benefits for the organization are:

- improved individual performance and, therefore, departmental performance
- improved efficiency and profitability
- improved quality of production and service
- a more accurate assessment of individual and departmental potential.

The benefits for you, as a manager, are the same as those for the organization, plus:

- improved communication and relationships with your staff
- identification of team weaknesses and strengths
- identification of existing and potential problems within the team
- identification of individual and departmental training needs

- finding out about your own strengths and weaknesses as a manager
- more opportunities to communicate departmental and company objectives
- opportunities to give and receive constructive feedback.

The benefits for those you manage are:

- an opportunity for individuals to express their own views about their present jobs
- an opportunity for them to find out about their own strengths and weaknesses
- an opportunity for them to discuss their own objectives
- an opportunity for them to discuss company and departmental objectives
- an improved working relationship with their managers.

The development review

These also take the form of a session involving a manager and an individual member of staff. The difference is that the purpose of the development review is to help that individual work through specific personal and professional development steps within the context of the organization's broader development policy, which in itself is related to the business plan.

The benefits for the organization are:

- an aid to successful planning
- a greater likelihood of retaining key people
- a recruitment aid that earns the company a reputation in the labour market as one that is committed to development
- higher staff awareness of the need to take responsibility for their own career development
- assistance with establishing a 'learning culture'
- encouragement of practices such as job rotation, work experience schemes, project work, internal secondments and so on
- information on the type of personal and professional development programmes that employees are asking for.

The benefits for you, as a manager, are:

- clarification of an individual's commitment to a future in the department and organization
- identification of an individual's commitment to learning and development
- assistance with succession planning in the department
- greater understanding between you and your people
- potential for improved communication.

The benefit for those you manage is that they have:

- a clearer idea of their skills, interests and values
- opportunities to examine the balance between their working life and non-working life
- opportunities to develop professionally and personally
- a chance to pause and review their direction in life
- opportunities to discuss long-term career options in the organization
- a personal development plan.

Should performance reviews and development reviews be separated?

Some performance review systems attempt to deal with the individual's further career development. A few attempt to deal with the even broader aspect of his or her personal and professional development. If both the member of staff and the manager are focused on the member of staff's present job, it is very difficult for either to stand back and look at the bigger picture of that person's overall career and life perspective

The focus of each session is different. The primary focus of the performance review is the organization and what is required to help it achieve its business plan, whereas the primary focus of the development review is the individual and what is required to help him or her achieve personal and professional goals within the context of the business plan.

It is very difficult for both parties to change gear in a discussion and move the focus from the organization to the individual.

The preparation for each is different for both manager and employee, and the outcome is different. The performance review will produce a set of performance criteria; the development review will produce a set of personal and professional learning goals encapsulated in a development plan.

Table 2.1 summarizes some of these differences. A logical conclusion is that it is best to separate the performance review from the development review.

Table 2.1 ***Performance/development reviews***

	Performance review	**Development review**
Primary focus	Organization's needs	Individual's needs
Time interval	Six to twelve months	Six months to five years
Outcomes	Performance criteria for existing job	Personal and professional development goals encapsulated in a plan
Preparation	Business and departmental assessment	Self-assessment
Primary manager skills required	Giving constructive feedback and coaching; goal setting and action planning	Counselling; goal setting and action planning
Primary team member skills required	Receiving feedback; action planning; contracting	Self-assessment; research; goal setting and action planning; making decisions

The development plan

We believe strongly that it is the review process that is crucial for personal and professional development. The paperwork is incidental. However, there does need to be some recording and it is important that the paperwork reinforces the development philosophy and does not dictate the process.

A development plan, as a result of the guided discussion between a manager and a member of his or her staff, is the practical output of a development review. It should contain a list of agreed learning objectives that specify clearly:

- what is to be learned
- why the learning is to be undertaken – is it primarily personal or professional?
- whether it contributes to the business plan and, if it does, in what way
- when the learning will begin and when it should be completed
- what resources will be required
- where it will take place
- how it will be assessed.

Review this list against your own organization's development plan, if there is one. Are any elements missing?

The vision of the 'learning organization' is an organization that is continually expanding its capacity to create its future.

Peter Senge

Preparing for a development review

Before conducting a development review with a member of staff, you will need to provide them with a copy of the section of this chapter beginning 'How to get the most out of your development' through to the end of the chapter (pages 49–66).

In preparing for a development review, you should refresh your own understanding of the process by reading those sections yourself. It introduces people to the 70/30 rule and the idea of shared responsibility. It is also designed to get them to think more laterally and creatively about their careers and their overall personal and professional development. It describes the development review process and highlights what is in it for them and for the company. It gives them some tips on how to get the most out of the session and some guidance sheets to help them organize personal data and think through the issues that they may wish to raise with you.

Interviewer's guide

Prior to the review

- Familiarize yourself with the process. Your interviewee will be very well prepared. Are you? You will be facing a person who has done a great deal of thinking about themselves and their future. In one way this will make your task easier, but it will also be much more challenging.
- Check that each of your interviewees has booked a personal and professional development review with you. If not, ensure that a session is booked. Do not cancel or postpone the appointment. Agree a starting time and an anticipated finishing time. If more time is needed, a further session could be scheduled after the initial one.
- Review data on the interviewee. Consult any other performance appraisal information, succession plans and so on. Talk to colleagues and senior managers who know the person. If necessary, talk to the present management if your interviewee is currently on assignment away from their home base.
- Be clear about future needs for your own department and familiarize yourself with any plans for future developments. Decide what you may want and what you can offer in your own department in the future.
- Be familiar with those in the organization who can supplement your knowledge of other areas.
- From your knowledge of the person, try to anticipate what he or she may want to know about future options.
- Be clear about your objectives. What do you want to get out of the personal and professional development review? Can you be certain that you really are prepared to focus on helping the interviewee clarify his or her position, or might you be trying to satisfy a human resource need of your own?
- Allow sufficient time and ensure that there will be no interruptions. You probably need to allow about an hour. You

should ensure that your telephone is switched off and that people are aware that you are not to be interrupted.

During the review

As an overall guideline, you should not be doing more than 30 per cent of the talking. The purpose is to get the member of staff thinking and talking.

You might find it helpful to think of the review as consisting of four stages. These are not rigidly identifiable, but describing them can help you to structure the session.

- Stage 1 – Establishing the contract.
- Stage 2 – Exploring and clarifying.
- Stage 3 – Constructive feedback.
- Stage 4 – Action planning.

Stage 1 – Establishing the contract

'We have until ..., if we do need more time we can arrange for another session. The objective is to give you an opportunity to examine your own personal and professional development needs and to see what role the company and I can play in helping you satisfy those needs.' Make it clear that the interviewee should feel free to show you any summary charts or notes but that they are under no obligation to do so.

Stage 2 – Exploring and clarifying

Your task at this stage is primarily to help the interviewee to talk through and explore issues, concerns or ideas generated by the pre-review work. You will need to listen actively to understand the interviewee's present job situation and then to help explore the alternatives and options. At this stage you are also collecting data that will be useful in action planning. For example, how mobile is the interviewee prepared to be in the future? How much of their own time are they prepared to give to their development? How much company time do they expect to be given over to their development? You will also be helping them examine their motives for wanting a particular course of action. For example: 'Exactly why would you like to move into that area of work?'; 'Is it really a promotion that you want?'; 'What is underlying that ambition?'; 'Are there alternative ways of getting what you want?'

In behaving this way you will be demonstrating one of the four essential behaviours referred to elsewhere – open thinking. One of your aims during these reviews should be to encourage your interviewees to think more openly and laterally. Simply by using the skills listed below, you will be empowering them to think for themselves and develop greater confidence in their ability to take more responsibility for their own development.

Table 2.2 *Objective interviewer*

Do	Don't
Listen	Negate or devalue what the other thinks or says
Maintain eye contact	Pass judgement
Ask open questions	Interrupt
Summarize	Jump to conclusions
Get the person to focus	Display impatience
Check for understanding	Ask closed questions
Get the person to be specific	Ask multiple questions
Challenge inconsistencies – things that don't hang together	

Stage 3 – Constructive feedback

You may well find yourself in the position of having to give feedback, including negative – but always constructive – feedback. Sometimes people will express wishes that you believe or indeed know to be unrealistic. Be careful. Do you really know or do you simply believe it to be unrealistic? Your staff member may express an ambition in relation to your own department that you know you cannot support. Part of the new open culture is to be upfront and tell people clearly and openly about things that might be challenging for them to hear. If you are managing the interviewee's performance well, then there should be no big surprises but, on the other hand, the pre-review work may have stimulated ideas and ambitions new to the person as well as new to you.

Here are some tips on how to give constructive feedback and, in particular, how to manage the process of making negative feedback as constructive as possible.

1 *Be clear about what you want to say in advance*. Practise if necessary. Start with the positive. Most people need encouragement, to be told when they are doing something well. When you offer positive feedback, it helps the recipient to hear first what you appreciate about them or what they have done well. If you have something negative to convey, you could preface it and put it into context by saying, 'I really liked how you handled ... However, I think that you could have ...'. Our culture tends to emphasize the negative. The focus is likely to be on mistakes more often than on strengths. In a rush to criticize you may overlook what you liked. If the positive is registered first, any negative input is more likely to be listened to and acted on.
2 *Be specific*. Avoid general comments, which are not very useful when it comes to developing skills. Statements such as 'You were brilliant!' or 'It was awful!' may be pleasant or dreadful to hear, but they do not give enough detail to be useful sources of learning. Illustrate what the person did that led you to use the label 'brilliant' or 'awful'. Specific feedback offers more opportunity for learning.
3 *Select priority areas*. Don't save it all up and give the person a 'bumper bundle', especially if there is a great deal of negative feedback to be given.
4 *Refer to behaviour that can be changed*. It is not helpful to give a person feedback on something over which he or she has no control. For example, 'I really don't like your face/your height/the colour of your eyes' and so on is not offering information that the person can do anything about.
5 *Offer alternatives*. If you do offer negative feedback, then don't simply criticize, but suggest what the person could have done differently. Turn the negative into a positive

suggestion: 'The fact that you remained seated when Anne came in seemed unwelcoming. I think if you had walked over and greeted her, it would have helped put her at ease.'

6 *Be descriptive rather than evaluative.* Tell the person what you saw or heard and the effect that it had on you, rather than merely saying that something was 'good' or 'bad'. Saying 'Your tone of voice as you said that really made me feel that you were concerned' is likely to be more useful than 'You were unhelpful'.

7 *Own the feedback.* It is often easy to say to the other person 'You are ...', suggesting that what follows is a universally agreed opinion. In fact, all you are entitled to give is your own experience of that person at a particular time. It is important that you take responsibility for the feedback you offer. Beginning the feedback with 'I' or 'in my opinion' is a way of avoiding the impression of being the giver of 'cosmic judgements' about the other person.

8 *Leave the recipient with a choice.* Feedback that demands change or is imposed on the other person may invite resistance and is not consistent with the belief that everyone is personally autonomous and has 'individual sovereignty'. It does not involve telling a person what he or she must do to suit you. Skilled feedback offers people information about themselves in a way that leaves them with a choice of whether to act on it or not. Ideally, it should help examine the consequences of any decision to change or not to change, but should not prescribe change.

9 *Think what it says about you.* Feedback is likely to say as much about the giver as the receiver. It will say a good deal about your values and what you focus on in others, so you can learn about yourself if you listen to the feedback you give.

10 *Remember the cultural context.* In some cultures it is difficult to give negative feedback because people are considered to lose face. In others, positive feedback can cause acute embarrassment. It is important to temper feedback according to cultural expectations.

Making negative feedback as constructive as possible

When you have to tell people something that you know they might find difficult or painful to hear, you may have a number of concerns:

1 Will they get very upset and, if so, how do I deal with it?
2 Will it affect the relationship I have with that person in any lasting way?
3 Will they hear what I am saying or will they distort it?
4 Will it have any effect on the way they behave?

Let's examine each of these concerns in turn.

1 *Will they get very upset and, if so, how do you deal with it?* People will often avoid telling someone else unpleasant things because it can make them feel bad when they do it, or sometimes they find it uncomfortable to have to cope with another person's distress or anger. An essential question to ask yourself in this situation is, 'Can I afford not to give the feedback?'. Failure to give people negative feedback can result in:
   - no change in the person's behaviour because they don't know that it is causing difficulties
   - unrealistic expectations about personal or professional development opportunities in the company
   - an enormous confrontation in the future as things escalate
   - problems in your continuing relationship with the person, which naturally develop when you are aware of something and they are not or when you are trying to keep something from them. Giving them the feedback gives them an opportunity to change.
2 *Will it affect your relationship with that person in any lasting way?* The short answer is that it might! This is always a risk. You can minimize that risk by:
   - having a good relationship to begin with
   - giving the feedback in a skilled way
   - keeping the feedback specific (focused on the behaviour that is producing the problem).

Relationships are not magical or mystical conditions that happen only by accident of birth or good fortune. Relationships are good because people work at them. Feedback can be constructive if you remember a few basic guidelines and if it is given within the context of a good relationship.

3 *Will they hear what you are saying or will they distort it?* You can check if you have been accurately heard by asking the person to summarize what you have said to them and by giving them an opportunity to comment on what you have said.
4 *Will it really have any effect on how they behave?* This depends first on whether they accept the feedback or not. In the final analysis, people must make their own decision whether or not to accept the feedback. If they don't accept it, it is vital to clarify the limitations that this may place on their future development. Sometimes the person accepts the feedback but then does nothing to change their behaviour. This will usually be because the feedback was concluded without clear objectives to work to, and without a step-by-step action plan to enable the person to establish those objectives.

All too often, as managers, we forget to give positive feedback and avoid giving negative feedback.

Stage 4 – Action planning

This is the time to see what you can both agree on for the individual's personal and professional development in the job, in the department, in the organization and elsewhere in the company. You will need to complete the personal and professional development plan, an example of which can be found at the end of the chapter. The member of staff should have received a blank copy before the review. The plan can be completed during the session, or the interviewee can take it away to fill in and return to you. You will keep a copy of this and another copy will be kept by the interviewee. You could arrange a date in six months' time for a further review of progress.

The remainder of this chapter has been written so that a copy of it can be handed, in its entirety, to members of staff to help them prepare for a development review.

How to get the most out of your development review

Development – a shared responsibility

What can a personal and professional development review provide for you?

Here is Edward Bear, coming downstairs now, bump, bump, on the back of his head behind Christopher Robin. It is, as far as he knows, the only way of coming downstairs, but sometimes he feels there really is another way, if only he could stop bumping for a moment and think of it.

A.A. *Milne*, Winnie the Pooh

Unfortunately, Edward Bear's experience is not an unfamiliar one for many people. The 'dailyness' of everyday life can often mask vague dissatisfaction with one's job, career and life in general, or sometimes even significant feelings of frustration. This is why it is vital to stop occasionally to review and reflect. A development review will provide you with such an opportunity.

There is a game that people often play called 'Things will be different when ...'. Which of these are you waiting for before you make your next career decision?

- passing your exams
- a new job
- a promotion
- a salary rise
- buying your first house
- moving house
- getting married
- having children
- your children leaving home
- retiring.

What else are you waiting for? How will things be different? Does all of this sound familiar to you?

The habit of waiting for things to happen can develop early. Months and then years can go by like this, even entire lives. To break the pattern and to take charge of your life, it is important to believe and to demonstrate that:

- there is always an alternative
- tomorrow need not be like today
- you don't have to be ill to get better.

There are 168 hours in each week. For someone of 30, with an average life expectancy of 75 years, that comes to a total of 393 120 hours left to live. With such a huge investment of time (an ever-decreasing resource), it seems not unreasonable to ask a few questions. Take some time to consider your answers now:

What results do I want from the efforts I make in my life?

What results am I getting from the way I spend my time at the moment?

At the end of my life, what will I need to have done to be able to say to myself, 'That was the best way I could have invested those hours'?

These questions are not easy to answer. You will probably need to return to them several times before you feel comfortable with your conclusions. By the time you have had your development review, you should be better able to answer them.

Your role in development

You are your own career manager – the 70/30 rule

The company wants you to have the opportunity to develop and grow professionally and personally, and believes that it has a responsibility to help you do that. Primarily, however, the responsibility must lie with yourself. You know best what you want. The company can make suggestions and give you information, opportunities and feedback on how you are perceived. But in the final analysis you are the person who needs to:

- know what you want from the company
- know what you are prepared to contribute
- create opportunities for yourself.

So 70 per cent of the responsibility lies with you, 30 per cent with your company. Be creative and remember, 'Up is not the only way'. You can move sideways as well as down.

Career patterns

The word 'career' means different things to different people. It is easy to assume that other people's thinking is the same as yours. This is obviously not so. The patterns and models that people work to, what is important to them and the needs they want to meet in their work and their lives are as unique to each person as are their fingerprints. That is why self-awareness, particularly in the areas of your needs and ambitions, is an important part of professional development. Children are subject to influences and conditioning that shape their lives and their view of life as they grow up. As adults their ideas of what is 'normal' affects their thinking and behaviour. Everyone has a set of beliefs about jobs and work and careers that influences the way they approach their own development.

What has been your career pattern and style? Do you:

1 Move from job to job with no particular direction?
2 Pursue status?
3 Prize independence and flexibility?
4 Stick with the job or career you selected early in life?
5 Prefer job satisfaction to promotion?
6 Seek promotion/career advancement within your field?
7 Move from career to career?
8 Value variety, creativity and personal growth over advancement and status?

Read on to find out about your career pattern.

Michael Driver, a career-development researcher in the USA, has suggested that, while everyone is unique and has an individual approach to career development, there do seem to be some basic career patterns that people follow. There are no right or wrong career patterns, just different ones that fit and work for different people. His research suggests four basic patterns, each of which has three key elements relating to:

- the time of life when the career choice is made
- the permanence of the choice
- the direction of the career change.

Someone following a *horizontal pattern* makes no permanent choice about jobs or career fields, but moves from job to job with no particular direction. There is no pursuit of higher status. The primary motivation for this person is independence and he or she is likely to be flexible by nature. (See questions 1, 3 and 8 above.)

Those with a *steady-state career pattern* select a job or career field early in life and then stay with it. Such people like the security of a 'job for life' and are likely to seek job satisfaction rather than promotion, although they do sometimes move for higher income or to a position requiring more of their professional skills. (See questions 2, 4 and 5 above.)

The *vertical career pattern* is one in which a career path is chosen early in life. That career path is adhered to but the pursuit is of upward advancement within that particular field. This vertical development can be through an organizational hierarchy or within a profession, but essentially those following this pattern are pursuing achievement, status, power and material success. (See questions 2, 4 and 6 above.)

The *cyclical pattern* is followed by those who become involved in a particular career field for a certain time but then leave it to enter another field that may or may not be related. This new field will also occupy the person for a time but then there will be another switch and immersion in yet another career area. The cyclical pattern of career development is composed of a series of phases, each lasting five to ten years. Advancement or status does not mean a great deal to those following such a pattern, who are attracted more by variety, creativity and the personal growth attained by wider experience. (See questions 3, 7 and 8 above.)

The vertical career pattern has been prominent in recent years. In hierarchical or growing organizations it is obviously possible for many people to achieve promotion. However, as companies change their structure and become flatter and leaner, then vertical careers become more difficult to maintain as a realizable concept for everyone. Many managers in British industry will not achieve promotion. 'Plateaued' managers, those who are not going to be promoted, can become demotivated and less effective as a result. There is a real need currently for people to recognize that their own development, creativity and life satisfaction may require them to switch career patterns if their previous one ceases to be feasible. In our fast-changing business and economic future, the cyclical pattern is likely to become significantly more common.

This can actually be very liberating once we have got used to the idea. Not everyone wants to be at the top of the management hierarchy, and there are increasing opportunities in companies for broadening your experience, developing new interests, learning new skills, working on new projects and taking on a variety of responsibilities. Some hurdles may be put in your way by the company, but you will have erected some yourself.

Don't be worried about changing your career plans. Between young adulthood and middle age (say a 20-year period) people have been shown to change 52 per cent of their interests, 55 per cent of their career interests, 69 per cent of their self-rated personality characteristics and 92 per cent of their answers to questions about their attitudes. The research demonstrating this was carried out in 1955. What would the equivalent research show today with the more dramatic rate of social and economic change?

All too often people set goals for themselves in their teens or twenties. Then they age and develop, but are still working towards goals which may no longer be appropriate to the people they have become.

Having arrived doesn't mean much if you're bored getting there!

Look at the career patterns matrix in Table 2.3 and then review how you've changed – and are still changing.

Table 2.3 *Career patterns matrix*

Type of career	When choice of pattern is made	How often occupations are changed	Direction of change	Motive for choosing this pattern
Horizontal variety	Never. People do not consciously make a choice	1–2 years	Levels are not relevant	Variety, challenge, 'doing what you want to regardless'
Steady, 'more of the same'	Young adult	Never or rarely, forced	Stays the same	Security, intrinsic job satisfaction, wanting a job for life
Vertical, 'the ladder'	Young adult	Never or rarely unless forced Jobs are changed for advancement	Upwards	Achievement, status, material success, power
Cyclical, 'the five-year itch'	Every 5–10 years	5–10 years	Levels are irrelevant	Variety, personal growth

Which career pattern do you want? Look at the matrix and answer the following questions:

Which career pattern is closest to the one you are currently pursuing?

What rewards and satisfactions have you been seeking through this pattern?

Which is the closest to the one you would like in the future and why?

What would you gain from following this pattern?

How much have you changed?

Fill in the chart in Table 2.4 and review the implications of your answers. Is there a pattern guiding your progress?

Does this review help you focus more clearly on the questions concerning your career pattern?

Table 2.4 ***Career pattern chart***

	My activities outside work	My marital status	My two key priorities	My ambitions
10 years ago				
5 years ago				
Now				
5 years hence				

Summary

In this section you have looked at your role in guiding your own development and in deciding where you want to be. You have observed that it is natural to revisit and change your goals as you move on in life and have looked at the emerging pattern in your own life.

This preliminary thinking will serve as a starting point to help you to prepare for your development review.

Your development review

What can a development review provide for you? Your development review has been designed to give you an opportunity to look at where you are in your job and in your career with the company, as well as considering relevant personal issues. It is a chance for you to:

- think about your future
- collect data about yourself – your skills, your interests, what is important and unimportant to you and about work, your

preferred career pattern and the type of person you are
- find out what opportunities there might be for you in the company in the future
- think about how you like to learn and what resources are available to you to help you learn and develop
- discuss your development needs openly with your manager
- make suggestions as to how your manager and the company could help you develop
- produce a personal and professional development plan.

It is *not*:

- an opportunity to discuss particular work issues or problems related to your present job
- about salary issues.

What can development reviews do for the company?

You may now be wondering why the company is providing you with this opportunity. Take a moment to think about what the benefits may be for the company. This company firmly believes that its success is built on the skills, creativity and commitment of its people. We consider that we have a responsibility to help you develop both professionally and personally. We know what kinds of skills are needed to make ours a successful business. Through our performance management system, we have information about you and your career with us to date. What we have less information about is what you want from us. This review is a chance for an open exchange of views and information between your manager and yourself. In summary, the value to the company of holding development reviews is that:

- we have a clearer idea of what we can do to help you develop – which will be good news for us too!
- we are less likely to offer you inappropriate career opportunities
- we can give you realistic information about prospects with us
- you may identify needs within the company of which we are unaware.

Preparing for your development review and making the most of it

What follows are some tips that will help you to get the most out of your development review.

Before the review

You should have spent some time collecting important data about yourself that will help you make decisions about how you want to develop next, both personally and professionally. It is extremely useful if you have some clear ideas on these topics before the development review, so make some notes below each heading.

What you're good at – your skills:

What you enjoy doing – your interests:

What you need to work on – your development needs:

What is important to you about work – your values:

What kind of career path you hope to follow – your career pattern:

It is extremely useful to summarize some data about yourself that will give both you and your manager a picture of the type of person you are and the way in which you might wish to develop yourself and your career in the future. To this end, it is suggested that you complete the personal summary sheet (Table 2.5) on the next page, as well as the personal and professional development at work summary that follows it (Table 2.6). Take these completed summaries with you to the review, together with any notes you have prepared and a list of any questions that you want answered.

The personal and professional development at work summary provides you with a list of opening lines that might serve as useful triggers for you. You can use this as a checklist of topics to cover during your review.

At the beginning of the review

- Establish exactly how long you have with your manager.
- State very clearly what you wish to gain from the session – your objectives.
- Ask your manager what he or she hopes to gain from the session.
- Ensure that you both fully understand what is going to follow.

Begin your review

- Present the summary of what you have realized about yourself from your personal summary sheet and personal and professional development at work summary sheet
- You may find it useful to structure your thoughts around the goals recorded in these summaries.

Table 2.5 *Personal summary sheet*

My main skills are:
My work interests are:
My work values are:
As a person my style is:
What I would like to do in the next 12 months is:
I learn best by:
My resources to help me learn and develop are:

Table 2.6 *Personal and professional development at work summary*

What I would like to do in the next 12 months is:

What I would like to do in the next 2–3 years is:

What I would like to do in the next 4 years and beyond is:

The contribution I could make to the company is:

What I would like from this job is:

I see my future in this department as:

I want to do the following in the next .... years:

What I would like to know from the company is:

What I would like to know from you is:

I would appreciate the following help from you/the company:

My resources to help me learn and develop are:

Other issues for me are:

During the review

Ask for feedback as you go along – don't hold the big questions back until the end:

- Ask your manager for reactions to what you have said.
- Ask for any data that he or she, or the company, has about you that is relevant to your career thinking.
- Ask for any data that he or she has about the company and its future that is relevant to you. Ask three specific questions: 'How do you see my future in this job?'; 'How do you see my future in this department?'; 'How do you see my future in this company?'

Make sure that you are clear about the answers you receive before the review ends to prevent any future misunderstandings or disappointments.

Remember the rules for receiving feedback:

- Listen to any feedback rather than immediately rejecting it or arguing with it. Feedback can be uncomfortable to hear, but you may be worse off without it. People may think something about you without telling you and then you are at a disadvantage. Others do have opinions of you and perceptions of your behaviour, and it can help to be aware of these. However, remember that you are also entitled to your opinion and you may choose to ignore the feedback as being of little significance, irrelevant or referring to behaviour that for some reason you wish to maintain.
- Be clear about what is being said. Avoid jumping to conclusions or becoming immediately defensive. If you do, people may cut down their feedback and you may not be able to use it fully. Make sure that you understand the feedback before you respond to it. A useful technique can be to paraphrase or to 'playback' any criticism to the giver, to check that you have understood.
- Check views of you with other people rather than relying on only one source of feedback. If others agree, you can be more sure that there is something to work on. If you rely on only

one source of feedback, then you may imagine that that individual's opinion is shared by everybody. In fact, if you check with other people you may find that their experience of you is different and you will have a more balanced view of yourself that will enable you to keep the feedback in proportion.

- Ask for the feedback you want but don't get. Feedback can be so important that you may have to ask for it if you don't come by it naturally. Sometimes you do get some feedback but it can be restricted to one aspect of your behaviour. You may have to ask that, in the future, you are given feedback that you would find useful but don't currently get.
- Decide what you will do as a result of the feedback. 'It takes two to know one.' You need to know how other people experience you to extend your self-awareness, which is incomplete if it is only your own version of yourself. We all need feedback to assist in our development and improve our effectiveness. When you receive it you can assess its value, the consequences of ignoring it or using it and, finally, decide what to do as a result. If it makes sense and adds up and you still do not make decisions on the basis of it, then the feedback may be wasted.
- Finally, thank the person for giving the feedback. You might benefit from it, it may not have been easy for the person to give and this is a valuable practice to reinforce in any organization or relationship.

Objective setting for development – at the end of the development review

- Decide what you can agree on – for you personally, for you in your present job, for you in the department, for you in the company.
- Next, set some personal and professional development objectives: for example, 'I want to spend less time sorting out team problems and more time on important paperwork'. You should aim for three to five objectives. Your personal objectives should state simply what you want to achieve. They should not describe how you will achieve them – that is an action plan. It is important that your objectives are not only clear and simple, but realistic.

Eleven steps to clear objectives

When you have decided on your development objectives, run them through the following 11-step process, answering the questions. When you have done this, you should aim to have three to five clearly defined and realistic objectives.

1. State your objective clearly – start with the word 'To …' followed by an action word. For example: 'To master a word-processing programme and learn keyboard skills.'
2. Ask yourself whether there is an objective behind your objective. Ask why you want what you want. There may be other ways of getting it: for example, if you are pursuing responsibility, status or extra money there may be other ways of achieving it without actually being promoted.
3. State clearly how you will know when your objective has been reached – this will ensure that your objective is clear.
4. Make your objective as specific as possible: for example, not 'I want my life to be more rewarding', but 'I want to get more satisfaction from my job by …'
5. State when you want to achieve this by and why you have chosen that date: for example, 'I want to achieve promotion by this time next year, because to wait longer would be frustrating'.
6. Be clear that you really want this for yourself and not just to please someone else.
7. Check whether any of your objectives conflict. For example, if you have said that you want to work for more responsibility but also that you want to spend more time with your family, then you have to decide whether these two objectives are compatible. If any of your objectives conflict then you will obviously have to identify which ones have priority and work on those.
8. Identify any constraints (external or internal) that will make your objective more difficult to achieve.
9. Identify any resources (external or internal) that will assist in the achievement of your objective.
10. Check that your objective is realistic. As before, talk it through with someone else (or with several other people)

who can provide useful alternative perspectives on how to tackle it

11 Ask whether there is anything to stop you achieving your objective now. If not, you are ready to start. However, if there are obstacles, then obviously you have as an initial objective to work to overcome those particular constraints.

This process can be repeated for any number of objectives.

Completing your review

Fill in the personal and professional development plan with your manager. This can be found overleaf. If this is not possible at the end of the session, then you can take the form away with you to complete. This should be done as soon as possible after the session.

After the review

- Ensure that you have a summary of what you have agreed.
- Start work on your action plan using your personal summary sheet and your agreed objectives as well as any other resources you may have, and make your future as you want it to be.
- Think about whether your answers have changed at all as a result of your review.

Summary

In this section you have looked at the value of a development review for your company as well as for you. You have also looked in detail at how you can prepare for your review and get the most out of it while you are there.

Table 2.7 ***Personal and professional development plan***

Name: ______________________________

Date: ______________________________

Manager: ______________________________

Development objectives	How they support business plan	Professional/personal	By when	Success criteria	Learning activities	Venue	Resources required	Relevant dates

Signed by manager ______________________ Employee ______________________ Head of unit/company ______________________

3

Manager as Coach

Of the range of strategies available to you as a manager for developing your people, perhaps the most significant will be the process of coaching.

Those teams that have been most successful are the ones who have demonstrated the greatest commitment to their people. They are the ones who have created the greatest sense of belonging. And they are the ones who have done most in-house to develop their people.

Bill Walsh, Head Coach San Francisco 49ers, 'Team of the Decade', quoted in the Harvard Business Review, *February 1993*

Perhaps the most important measure of your effectiveness as a manager is your ability to elicit quality performance from those who report to you. On the way to achieving your management position, the focus is likely to have been on your own work performance or your area of technical expertise. As you have advanced, the focus has probably switched to your ability to lead a group of others towards superior performance.

One manager described that experience: 'Once I was an outstanding research chemist, now I have little time for my own research. My job is to enable about 60 others to carry out quality research for the good of themselves, the organization, and eventually those who will use what we discover.' From being an individual contributor to the company, she was now in a position to benefit it even more, through the people she managed and led.

What is coaching?

Coaching is:

Developing the competence and experience of others, in a planned and progressive way, by offering guidance and challenge through a series of learning activities, with review and feedback to support and reinforce the learning.

At some stage of our development, we have all probably experienced learning through being coached, although it may not have been called coaching. If we look at the definition above, it covers what we have experienced when we have:

- been taught to drive a car, ride a bike or sail a boat
- had music lessons, or been taught to play a musical instrument
- been taught sporting skills – tennis, swimming, cricket, skiing and so on
- learned the skills involved in taking up a new job.

In what other circumstances have you developed through being coached? It will be useful just for a moment to reflect on what we might learn from our previous experiences of coaching: about the process itself and the skills of the 'coach' (for example driving instructor, music teacher, sports coach).

Pick one experience in which you have learned from being coached, think it through and ask yourself:

Was my 'coach' effective (or not) in helping me learn quickly and effectively? Why?

What impressed me – what did the 'coach' do that helped me learn, or perhaps hindered or slowed my learning?

Did my 'coach' teach me a lot of theory before I did anything or did practice come first, or were the two interspersed?

Was my 'coach' an expert performer or just a good teacher, or both?

Was my learning 'one step at a time' or 'in at the deep end'?

Did my 'coach' use criticism more than encouragement or vice versa? What motivated me to want to learn?

What does my reflection tell me will be most important for me to remember when I am coaching others in the future?

What did you realize? Probably that you have received a fair amount of 'coaching', one way or another. It is also highly likely you will have experienced some 'coaches' who were more successful in helping you learn than others. That realization will be helpful in making you aware of some of the skills that matter and will make you an even more successful coach in the future.

You may have also realized the following:

- It is possible for a learner to discern what makes a good coach and what doesn't. We do learn better from some people than from others.
- Some theory can help learning (we can read books or watch videos on how to drive a car or play golf, and so on), but most learning comes from doing rather than hearing, and in most cases learning involves both theory and practice.
- Sometimes we learn a lot from experts, but sometimes experts are not good coaches (some of the top sports performers regularly go to little-known coaches who 'straighten out' their technique, although these coaches do not play to a high standard themselves). We can be good coaches without being top performers if we know the subject, are credible and the learner has confidence in us.
- 'In at the deep end' is one way to learn, but it is rarely the most effective and can sometimes result in a loss of confidence and in confusion that can block later learning. 'One step at a time', progressively more challenging, building on what we have learned and then pushing on, is probably the most effective learning strategy.
- It is interesting to debate whether we learn best from criticism or from encouragement. There are some people who are so resentful of criticism that they bounce back and become even more motivated to learn. However, for many, criticism, especially if it is felt to be unfair or uncaring, is significantly less of a motivator than genuine encouragement and constructive feedback.
- We will have been motivated to learn by different factors at different times. Sometimes it is pride in our own achievement that drives us to learn, sometimes it is a wish for advancement, promotion or greater status, sometimes it is for material gain, sometimes for the approval of somebody we value. Whatever the source or type, however, it is likely that motivation will have played a significant part in all our learning.

What has motivated your learning? Reflect on one or two of your main skills or areas of expertise and identify your motivators (the reasons for you putting in the effort you did to achieve the learning).

Table 3.1 ***Motivators for learning***

Skill or area of learning	Why I learned it

What are your current motivators for working through this book? Pay-offs do not need to be material gains. Greater self-confidence and self-satisfaction are legitimate pay-offs for an investment in learning. What will the benefits or pay-offs be for investing your time and energies in further development to become a more effective coach?

The benefits of coaching

Coaching is regularly a win–win–win process. The learner clearly benefits, but so does the coach and so does the organization of which they are a part. Let's pause and appreciate why coaching is such a valuable process. Why is it such a good investment of time and energy to help your staff towards greater and greater competence?

Think about the benefits that you believe might result from an effective coaching programme, and then consider the suggestions that follow to see how they tally with your ideas.

The benefits of coaching for the learner, or member of staff:

For the coach, or manager:

For the organization:

Below are the commonly recognized benefits. See how your ideas match up with these. Tick the points that you agree with.

For the learner:

- Greater competence and confidence resulting in better performance, and perhaps eventually in greater status and greater reward.
- Greater readiness to take on further development resulting from, and in, greater self-esteem.
- More confidence in management and the organization resulting from appreciation of the development opportuni-

ties provided (some research suggests that people are more loyal to organizations that support their development).

- Greater independence resulting from greater competence and greater readiness to take on new challenges.
- Increased job satisfaction resulting from better all-round performance.

For you, the coach:

- Improved work team performance that results from more competent staff, and improved quality of performance that comes from getting more things right first time.
- Possible reduction of management time spent problem solving.
- Increased self-esteem from seeing people 'blossom' under your guidance, plus more flexibility of staff and more of a 'team' approach to work.
- Enhanced reputation as a manager, deriving both from your team's performance and from your role as a developer of people, resulting in turn in increased potential for your own advancement in status or reward.
- Increased skill development, expansion of your own competences, more time for your own development because your people are more competent and, potentially, more job satisfaction.

For the organization:

- Greater all-round effectiveness and productivity resulting from more competent staff, plus greater awareness of the talent within the organization, its potential and its needs.
- Improved quality of work, for the same reason, resulting in less waste of time and, possibly, of materials.
- Enhanced reputation as an employer where people get on, more trust in the workplace.
- Savings, from owning your own talent rather than having to buy it in and from doing more with the same resources.

Did you agree? Were there benefits that you identified that were not listed? If there are so many benefits, why do some managers fight shy of spending time on coaching their staff, and what is it in some organizations that prevents coaching being used productively as a means of staff development? Often it is a problem of time and the pressures of everyday problem solving and 'fire-fighting'. Less critical activities such as coaching can get lost along the way. We can also observe that very hierarchical organizations do not always make full use of coaching because it involves managers and their staff working side by side, on the same level, and this may contradict the hierarchy.

The obstacles to coaching

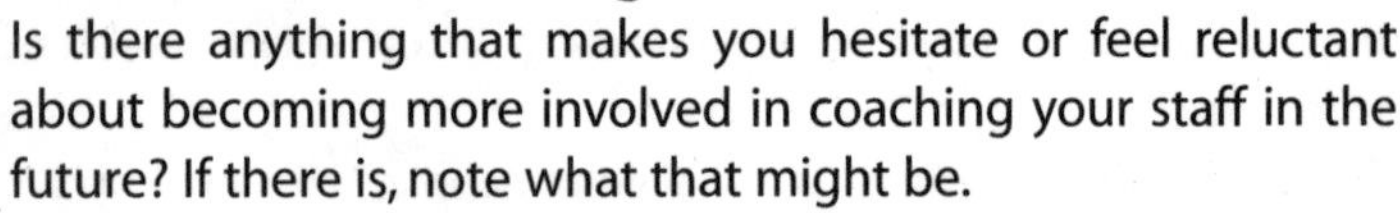

Is there anything that makes you hesitate or feel reluctant about becoming more involved in coaching your staff in the future? If there is, note what that might be.

Identifying a block or barrier can be the first stage in removing it or moving round it!

Here are some of the reasons that managers often give for not coaching their staff:

- I don't have time.
- They're just not interested.
- I'll delegate it.
- There isn't anyone who can do it.

The concerns about coaching are usually the same as those about delegation – the most immediate being time. Coaching is the first step to successful delegation. It is a long-term investment. It does initially take longer than doing the job yourself, but it will be possible to delegate similar tasks to that person again and again and so reserve your own time for other activities. We need to break the 'vicious circle' of continuing to do everything ourselves and never having enough time for our really important responsibilities. Once we have broken that circle, things become much easier. We will have freed ourselves to do more coaching in different areas, which in turn frees us to do other things.

Other common concerns that managers have are:

- *The element of risk.* 'Nobody will do it as well as I could myself.' This is likely to be true in the early stages, but is a very short-term view. If people in the past had thought that and not coached you, then you would not be in the position you are in today. Besides that, hanging on to expertise, not developing others, could mean you having to cope with an ever-increasing workload and with staff who are resentful of your lack of trust in them, and that is a very stressful road. In a properly supervised coaching process the real risks are small and the potential is great!
- *Losing control of myself and my work.* Managers can only manage by consent. In the end, you can only be as good as the team you manage. Research shows that managers who delegate more and who develop the competences of their staff achieve more and are held in higher regard by those they manage and by the organization. When you develop your people, you also develop a good relationship with them and you then have more influence and control.
- *Losing some of the work that I am good at or enjoy.* Management is much more about overseeing work than doing it yourself. You may well lose some work that you enjoy, but you may also free yourself to do other work that you can also enjoy and that challenges you. You may be worried about moving into this hands-off management role, but without a readiness to do that there can be no progression in your development and career.
- *Losing staff through promotion to other departments, sections or companies.* Let's face it, this is also a possibility. Today, organizations and the managers and supervisors within them face a dilemma. If you develop people, you make them more marketable and they will be more attractive to other employers. If you don't develop them, they are unlikely to want to stay with you in any case, and you will probably not be getting

value for money from them even if they do. Besides, coaching spreads the expertise. It means that you are not putting too many eggs into one basket. Once you start the coaching process, there will always be other people ready to carry on where a departing employee has left off. That is a route to greater security, because security comes from always having an alternative.

What does coaching give you?

Read through the checklist in Table 3.2 and tick the first column of boxes from the coach's point of view.

Table 3.2 ***What does coaching give you?***

As coach	As learner	
		The satisfaction of knowing that you are doing a good job
		More confidence in your role and your skills
		Better relationships with your work team
		The feeling of being a professional
		More respect from your colleagues and your manager
		Better relationships with your manager
		Knowledge that your job is more secure
		Better promotion prospects
		Less boredom in your job

Now go through the list ticking the second column of boxes from the learner's point of view.

You are likely to find that you have ticked the same statements for each role. As we have said already, coaching is a win–win–win process.

If you have done some coaching previously, were any of these benefits missing from your previous experience? Look back over the list and consider any that you did not tick. What were the benefits that you missed out on? What might the reasons have been?

Benefit 1:

____

____

What might the reason(s) have been?

____

____

Benefit 2:

____

____

What might the reason(s) have been?

____

____

Benefit 3:

____

____

What might the reason(s) have been?

____

____

When you have completed this chapter you will probably be able to pinpoint the reasons that any previous coaching may not have seemed so fruitful. This awareness will help you ensure that you experience the benefits in future.

Summary

In this section we have looked at:

- what coaching is – an overview of the process and set of skills
- your previous experiences of coaching, as coach and learner

- what the benefits of coaching can be for the learner, coach and organization
- what the obstacles to coaching can be.

In the remainder of the chapter we will introduce the coaching process in detail and identify the coaching skills that support that process.

The coaching process

Coaching will be most effective when the process and the skills are understood, used naturally and applied directly to a real work situation. This chapter can be your 'coach' in the progress towards enhancing your skills, but at this stage you will need to identify someone to coach so that you can gain some practical experience. That should not be difficult to do if you are already a manager, because coaching somebody in your work team will be a natural place to start. Failing that, you might choose a less experienced colleague looking for expertise or even somebody in a non-work situation (say a partner, a member of the family, a junior in a local sports club). You will need someone to coach to make the most of the rest of the chapter.

At the same time, you can learn a great deal from receiving coaching. Put yourself in the learning situation, either at work or outside (think of something that you would like to learn to do) and find a 'coach' to teach you. As you experience coaching from the receiving end, assess the process used and the skills of your coach against those described in the rest of the chapter.

The five stages of the coaching process

- Stage 1 – Identify the need and the opportunity.
- Stage 2 – Agree the goals and objectives.
- Stage 3 – Agree the learning steps.
- Stage 4 – Review.
- Stage 5 – Build on and restart.

Stage 1 – Identify the need and the opportunity
Coaching is about developing or extending somebody's knowledge or skill. In a work situation, it is not likely to be difficult to identify a need or to create an opportunity to coach. Common starting points can be:

- a newcomer who needs to be brought up to scratch in some area of expertise
- somebody whose current performance is causing problems
- a special project that will call for new skills from a member of staff
- a decision to delegate some area of responsibility to somebody to whom it will be new
- preparing somebody to cover for holidays or other periods of absence
- secondments to other departments or teams.

Whatever your situation, it should be a way of life for managers to be continually seeking opportunities to challenge and develop their staff further. What needs and opportunities can you see to apply the coaching process? Who could you coach to do what and what would be the benefits?

The need and opportunity for you to coach – describe who you should coach and in what.

____

____

The need and opportunity for you to receive coaching – from whom and in what?

____

____

Don't rush off yet and start the process; instead, further your awareness first.

Stage 2 – Agree the goals and objectives

This stage asks us to be clear about the results that we want (the goals) from the coaching process. For example, the goals in the process of learning to drive are that the learner should pass the driving test and be able to drive confidently and safely. Goals are important because:

If you don't know where you're going, you might end up somewhere else!

Goals keep our eyes and mind on where we want to get to, which gives us, and those we are coaching, a much greater chance of getting there. Objectives, on the other hand, are our means of getting there. There will be objectives for each stage in the coaching (learning) process. To use the example of learning to drive, the goal is clear but to get there we will need a course of lessons, each with learning objectives.

Our driving 'coach' might explain that the objectives for our first lesson are to become familiar with the controls of the car and the basic rules of the road. The objectives of the second lesson might be to learn to steer the car and perform basic gear changes. The third lesson could be to learn signalling, overtaking and how to make a right turn. You can see how objectives for each stage of coaching take us towards the goal.

Notice also that the word 'agree' is used in our title for Stage 2. It is all well and good for us, as a coach, to identify goals and objectives, but unless the learner is motivated to learn and achieve, then nothing will happen. Agreeing goals and objectives, getting the learner to 'own' them as their own goals and objectives, is essential for motivation. We will consider motivation later in the chapter.

Notice that goals and objectives usually start with the word 'to' followed by a verb (a word conveying action to be undertaken). For example, 'to learn …', 'to be able to …', 'to make …', 'to understand …'. Use that format when writing goals or objectives in your role as coach.

Let's use the process again.

What do you see as the goal(s) of the coaching you wish to

undertake, and what would be some of the intermediate objectives en route to them?

Goal(s):

Objectives – for the steps leading to the goal(s):

Who would you need to agree these with?

Stage 3 – Agree the learning steps

It is clear that significant coaching/learning goals are best approached in progressive steps. There are various steps to be accomplished before we will be able to drive a car competently and we need to be led through these, so that we don't have to learn everything at once or get things out of sequence. For example, it is apparent that we are better addressing three-point turns once we are familiar with clutch control and reversing, rather than vice versa.

For this reason, as you get further into planning your coaching assignment, you will be encouraged to look at the steps you wish the learner to undertake in pursuit of the overall skill or expertise. You will return to this stage as you prepare your assignment. For the moment, just focus on the five stages in the coaching process.

Stage 4 – Review

As learning develops we will need to check progress with the learner, so that:

- learning is consolidated
- we can check that the learner is comfortable and experiencing progress
- we can iron out any difficulties that may be occurring.

Reviewing is a key feature in any programme of learning!

Stage 5 – Build on and restart

There will be a need for you and the learner to accept that any coaching phase is only part of a never-ending journey of development. It is widely recognized now that learning is a life-long process. We can never afford to regard ourselves as 'fully developed', as able to 'insert a full stop'. Learning is not only necessary, it is also inevitable; it is part of simply being alive. Each episode of coaching equips the learner and the coach to appreciate what has been achieved, but also to see the achievement as a launchpad to further learning and further coaching.

So you have begun to:

- identify some coaching that you would like to undertake
- identify some goals and objectives for that coaching
- be familiar with the five stages in the coaching process.

Perhaps you feel that you would like to get underway now. It is wise not to rush off just yet, because it will make your coaching more fruitful if you pause to consider two more topics – how adults learn and the coaching skills needed to implement the five-stage process.

How adults learn

We have said that learning is a life-long process. Knowledge of how adults actually learn enables us to make the process easier and more successful. We need to consider three aspects:

- learning styles
- factors that help or hinder learning
- the learning curve.

Learning styles

We will coach more effectively if we are aware of the learning styles of those we coach. Each of us is unique, but we are also aware that there are some people who are 'more our type' than others. This is because there are basically four personality styles, each of which tackles things and learns in a particular way.

What is your learning style? Consider the questions in Table 3.3 overleaf. Total the number of ticks you have for each learning style. You are likely to have scores in each category, but your highest score will indicate your predominant learning style.

Now compare your scores to the descriptions of each style and reflect on which is most, and least, like your own preferred learning style.

Enthusiasts

Enthusiasts like new things, enjoy getting involved and especially working with people. They like talking and sharing ideas with others. They are less interested in detail, get bored easily and like 'doing' more than 'planning'. They prefer variety and can flit from task to task, although they are not always good at seeing things through. When they are interested they are completely involved; when they are not they will shy away and find reasons for not doing things. They like skim-reading rather than absorbing everything, and they don't like checking things through once they are finished. They are spontaneous, ask lots of questions and like new ideas and approaches.

Logicals

Logicals work systematically and can tackle subjects that they don't enjoy as well as those that they do. They are very thorough and will check details to ensure accuracy. They like to know the background and how things work. They like asking questions and solving problems. They like to complete one task before taking up another, and prefer to work through and get to the root of problems for themselves. They are organized and make lists, timetables and clear action plans. They prefer to listen rather than talk, like reading for ideas, studying for themselves and coming to their own conclusions.

Table 3.3 *Learning styles*

Do you:	Tick if yes
Get bored easily? Enjoy working in groups? Like to try out ideas on others? Like doing more than planning? Like variety and flitting between tasks? Skim-read rather than trying to absorb everything? Ask lots of questions? Enjoy new ideas and approaches?	
Total no. of ticks for 'Enthusiast' style	
Work systematically? Enjoy working in detail? Like to understand how things work and how ideas have been developed? Like finishing an activity before moving on to the next one? Prefer to work through problems for yourself? Like lists, timetables and action plans? Prefer to listen rather than talk? Prefer to study things for yourself?	
Total no. of ticks for 'Logical' style	
Like to spend a lot of time just thinking? Enjoy linking ideas and seeing connections? Like to find new ways of completing and presenting work? Work in bursts of energy? Like to float ideas with other people? Prefer diagrams to lists? Prefer the whole picture to detail? Enjoy challenging ideas?	
Total no. of ticks for 'Imaginative' style	
Like clear purpose and direction? Like to know what is required before starting a project? Know what is important to you and what you want to achieve? Like working on your own? Enjoy having targets and deadlines? Plan ahead and gather resources? Like charts and graphs that give data rather than attempt to be works of art? Work methodically and have timetables and agendas	
Total no. of ticks for 'Practical' style	

Imaginatives

Imaginatives are very reflective people, enjoying thinking sometimes more than actually getting down to work, especially written work. They are not very systematic. They are good at linking ideas together and seeing connections and enjoy finding new ways of completing and presenting work. They have bursts of energy and like to float ideas around with other people. They work creatively and prefer inventive diagrams to lists. They like seeing the whole picture, rather than detail, and they enjoy challenge and ideas.

Practicals

Practicals enjoy having a clear purpose and direction. They like planning, targets and knowing what's required when they start a project. They are clear about what is important to them and what they want to achieve. They prefer to work on their own, getting on with things and not being distracted or sidetracked. They like deadlines and organize themselves to achieve these, being impatient of those who fail to meet them. They plan ahead, gather the resources they need for any task and love data, especially in lists and charts and graphs. They follow instructions, work methodically and very much enjoy completing a task.

It is likely that you found one learning style that was most like you, with bits and pieces of the others also describing you. Please be aware that these are shorthand versions of the styles, and that there is definitely no right or wrong style. Each has its strengths and its shortcomings, and we all have something of each style in us. When we identify styles we are identifying a dominant style that is more apparent than the others.

The point of all this for a coach is that we need to be aware of the learning styles for those we coach and to plan our coaching programme accordingly. For example, with practicals we will need plenty of clear planning and direction, clear deadlines, concrete targets and so on. With enthusiasts, we will need more short-burst activity, more variety and innovation, more challenge to see things through and get results, and so on.

Think of your work team and those you will wish to coach. What different learning styles can you detect there and what will be the implications for the coaching that is ahead? Make a note of what occurs to you at this stage.

Factors that help or hinder learning

Let's be alert, not just to the different styles of those we will coach, but also to the 'helps' and 'hindrances' that support or block learning.

Off the top of your head, list the things that you see already that might assist or impede the learning of those you may wish to coach in the near future.

Read through the suggestions that follow, not just to check whether your answers are included, but also to raise your awareness of some of the factors to which all coaches need to be alert. You may have mentioned some of the following factors.

The starting point of the learner

Confidence is conducive to learning. It enables us to take on challenges, tackle problems and seek help if we need it. Sometimes we will be coaching people who have had their confidence about learning damaged by a lack of success in terms of formal learning, or because learning opportunities have not been part of their recent experience. They will need early success, challenges they can meet, before they address more difficult tasks. The coach must always balance support and challenge. Too much or too little of either will impede learning.

Motivation of the learner

It is sometimes said that we cannot motivate anybody; people choose to be motivated themselves. What we can do, however, is create circumstances that make it more likely that people will be motivated. Motivation is an individual matter. What spurs one person on will not appeal to another, so it will be a matter of identifying the pay-offs for learning that are attractive to the learners we coach. Pay-offs need not be material things: increased self-esteem, self-confidence, approval from somebody we respect, greater job satisfaction, all of these can be attractive gains from investing our time and energy in learning. But the bottom line is that learners must see benefits to motivate them to learn.

For a coach, the realization is that there are two sources of factors that can motivate the learner. The first are intrinsic factors in the learning process. That is, the process must be attractive, stimulating, varied, supported, challenging and generally impressive in itself. If it is, then it will be intrinsically motivating. In addition, there can be extrinsic factors that will motivate the learner. These might be such things as promotion, more pay, increased status, recognition or awards. When the learner can see gains that are appealing, then these can be extrinsically motivating.

Consider a piece of learning you have undertaken in the past. What were the motivators for you?

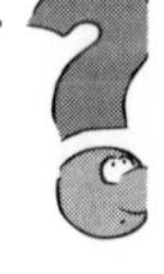

Intrinsic motivators:

____

____

Extrinsic motivators:

____

____

Think of somebody you might offer coaching to in the future. What might be the motivators for them?

Intrinsic motivators:

Extrinsic motivators:

Remember, however, that it is no good to us, as the coach, to believe that something should be a motivator unless the learner regards it as such.

Participation

Learning must involve the learner. It has to be an active process, requiring the learner to engage with the topic, absorb it, shape it, use it and see results from it. 'Sitting by Nellie', however talented Nellie is, can only ever be a tiny part of real learning. The learner needs eventually to be active and to take ownership of their learning.

A supportive situation

Learning happens best in environments that support the learner. These are usually free of interruptions, physically comfortable and attractive, with the necessary resources and equipment available.

How supportive to learning is the environment in which you will be coaching?

What might you do to make it more supportive?

The learning curve

Learning is not usually a story of steady, uninterrupted, even progress. We can prevent frustration in both the learner and the coach by being alert to what is known as the learning curve. The message in the theory is that early in any process of learning we are likely to experience rapid learning, which can be exciting and very satisfying. That rapid progress is then likely to be replaced by a period when the progress slows, when there can be a feeling of treading water, which is referred to as a 'learning plateau'. This can be disheartening and can sap the learner's (and the coach's) energy if it is not recognized as a normal part of the learning process. A change of focus, method or renewed incentives can all assist progress through the plateau, but the basic need is just to stay with it. Momentum and progress will return.

Rules of thumb

The following 'rules of thumb' are some simple ideas drawn from sound learning theory that are true most of the time, although experienced coaches will occasionally ignore the guidelines because they can see a better way.

- Coach from the known to the unknown – find the learner's starting point.
- Coach from the easy to the difficult.
- Coach from the practical to the theoretical.
- Coach from the part to the whole.
- Show the relevance and application of all learning.
- Have clear targets and 'milestones' to mark progress.
- Keep the momentum at a pace that just stretches the learner.
- Show results – nothing succeeds like success.
- Remember the learning curve.

Recall time

Before continuing, it is worth checking that you are clear about the ground we have covered so far in this chapter. This can be done by answering the following questions and then, before journeying on, check back to see whether there is anything that you may have missed.

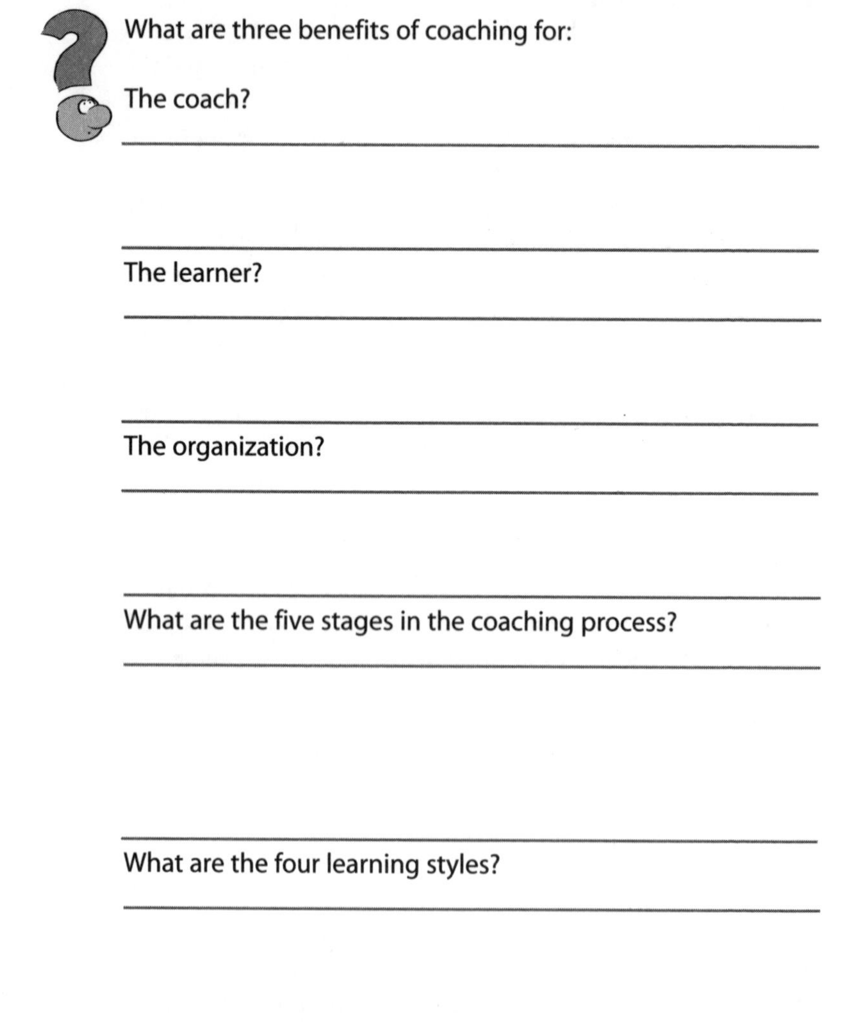

What are three benefits of coaching for:

The coach?

The learner?

The organization?

What are the five stages in the coaching process?

What are the four learning styles?

What helps and hindrances to learning should a coach be aware of?

Coaching skills

Soon we will ask you to design a coaching project to put your learning from this chapter into practice. Before that, it is valuable to focus on the coaching skills that support the process. These skills are important because they put the learner in charge of the learning.

The coach's job is to put him- or herself out of a job, in the sense that, through the coaching, the learner is eventually made independent of the coach. This involves always moving the process in the direction of putting the learner in control, making the learner take responsibility. For this reason, the coach operates in a non-directive style.

Figure 3.1 shows the progression from directive to non-directive styles.

Coaching styles

Directive		Non-directive
Coach in control		Learner in control
- - - - - - - - - - - - - - -	X - - - - - - - - - - - - - - -	Y
All coach		All learner

Coach/learner

Figure 3.1 ***Coaching styles***

Ideally, in most coaching activities the movement is between *X* and *Y*: from mutually agreed learning goals and methods to learner activity and achievement, to joint reviews back to further learner activity, until competence is reached. All the time the coach is analysing:

- Am I doing the work or is the learner?
- Am I making the learner think and work things out?
- Am I increasing the learner's independence?
- Does my contribution decrease as the learner's competence increases?

The coach's goal throughout is to oversee the process but not to take away the learner's ownership of it. The skills that allow this to happen are employed right through the five stages of coaching:

- cultivating a positive relationship
- creating a learning climate
- questioning
- reinforcing
- giving constructive feedback.

Let's consider these in more detail.

Cultivating a positive relationship

We learn best from coaches we like and respect. It is well known that the relationship between a teacher and a pupil will affect how well the pupil learns. This is also true of the coaching relationship. To be most fruitful, it must be a relationship in which the learner feels valued and respected by the coach. That means that the coach must communicate these feelings to the learner, both in words and in actions.

Write down five ways in which your own manager can make you feel valued and respected.

Reflect on what others have said about how they are made to feel valued and respected:

We feel valued and respected:

- *when people give us time and attention*
- *when they listen to us*
- *when they ask us our ideas*
- *when they smile and are relaxed with us*
- *when there are no 'airs and graces', sitting behind big desks, or hiding behind big titles*
- *when they are interested in our progress*
- *when they are encouraging and not critical*
- *when they show appreciation of our efforts*
- *when they challenge us to achieve more because they believe we are capable of more*
- *when they say 'well done' and mean it*
- *when their feedback is fair*
- *when they say 'thank you'.*

You have probably realized that these factors do not just concern coaching, they are about basic human relationships. All of us like to feel we are appreciated and valued, that we matter, and we respond positively when that is communicated to us. See whether your list matches with what others have said. There are many clues in your own list and in the suggestions above, but whatever your methods of communicating to those you coach that you value and respect them, the success you have will be related to the quality of the relationship that you build with the learner.

Creating a learning climate

We have already mentioned features of the physical environment that will encourage learning. Physical settings carry messages. Lighting, temperature, the layout of furniture, freedom from interruption, time available, comfort, provision of necessary resources can all be used to convey the message that coaching sessions are important and that the learner is valued and appreciated.

Consider again the physical setting in which you are likely to be coaching. What, if anything, is there in that setting that might need to be changed to make it more conducive to coaching and learning and what could you do to achieve that?

Questioning

Skilful questioning is perhaps the most valuable arrow in the coach's quiver. The key is to question in a way that makes the learner do the thinking, solve the problems and do the work. This type of questioning means asking open questions. These are usually short questions that lead to long, thoughtful answers from the learner. Examples might be:

- What do you want to achieve?
- What is success in your eyes?
- Why is that important?
- How will you achieve that?
- What options can you see?
- What are the next steps?
- What is the best way to tackle that?
- What have you learned from that?

Open questions such as these leave the work and the control largely with the learner and are greatly to be valued for that. As you apply your coaching skills, you will need to review your use of open questions and be conscious of the balance between challenge and support in your questioning. 'Be supportive' is the general rule, but do challenge when you feel that it will push the learner into further achievement. Questions that challenge might include:

- What else might you learn from that?
- Have you taken that as far as you can?

- Can you see a better way than that?
- Are you happy with the way that it's going?

Within a context of support, these questions and others like them will stretch the learner.

Reinforcing

Recognition is a powerful motivator. Telling somebody what they are doing well, showing appreciation of their achievements, reinforces the learning. Abilities that we have recognized become part of us because we use them more. If we hear ourselves genuinely praised for a quality displayed, we are likely to build it into our repertoire.

- The way you planned that and followed it through was excellent!
- You really do have a talent for writing accurate, precise reports!

Comments such as these, if they are genuine, will not only be music to the learner's ears, but will ensure that they make those qualities a consistent part of their performance.

Giving constructive feedback

You might recall a discussion in Chapter 2 concerning feedback. That discussion was, of course, in the context of conducting a development review, during which specific performance issues may need to be raised and the skills of giving negative feedback constructively become key to reaching a successful conclusion. It is relevant at this point to return to the subject of feedback, but this time considering it in the somewhat different context of the relationship between coach and learner.

Everybody can improve the quality of their performance by receiving constructive feedback from other people. There is an appropriate adaptation of an old saying that we mentioned earlier: 'It takes two to know one.' This suggests that knowing what other people think of us, knowing how they see our work, can help in our development. Basically, what feedback from other people does is to give us additional, valuable information. Rather than just having our own view of ourselves and our work, which is likely to be one-sided, we have other views and opinions to give us a more complete picture on which to act.

Feedback can help learners (and coaches) to adjust their performance towards higher-quality work. That will only be true, however, if the feedback is constructive and helpful. That is quality feedback!

Unskilful feedback can damage performance. Feedback that is overcritical, entirely negative or intended to punish rather than help can damage motivation and reduce the quality of learning. In a learning environment, feedback is used to develop learners and bring about continuous improvement in their work.

A coach can make feedback constructive in the following ways:

- *Always starting with the positive.* If we tell people genuinely what they do well, they will be much more ready to listen to what we believe they can do better. Unless people hear and accept the feedback, they will not use it. We have to keep them listening, hearing and motivated to want to change, and they will only do that if they feel that we respect them and are not writing them off.
- *Being specific and clear about what they should change.* Generalizations such as 'You are not very good, are you?' or 'You are just not up to it' are not very helpful because people are made to feel awful without knowing what or how to change. Saying 'I like your enthusiasm and keenness to please, but you will have to be very careful to make notes of the key steps every time' (or '...take careful notes of any phone messages' or '…ensure that every ledger entry is correct' and so on) lets the person know what to work on.
- *Asking what they think about what they have just been told.* We show respect by asking for their comments rather than the conversation being all one way. The person is more likely to act on the feedback if they feel that they have a chance to give their point of view.

- *Giving reasons for what you are asking.* Tell them what benefits will result from what you want them to change. People are more likely to respond to what they see as a reasonable request rather than an aggressive demand. So 'You must really make it a priority never to allow gaps on the shelves, because that costs us sales and looks unprofessional' is of a higher quality than 'Get those shelves filled, that's what you are paid to do'.
- *Providing feedback quickly and regularly.* Feedback that is stored up and then given long after something has happened is less effective than that given while circumstances are fresh in people's minds. Feedback should be a natural part of coaching and not treated as a special event.
- *Checking that the person has understood and now knows what is required of them.* Ask the learner to summarize what they will do as a result of the feedback and finish positively by reminding them of what they are doing well, pointing out that they now know what to do to become even more competent in the future.
- *Agreeing how you will review progress.* Setting objectives so that the person can use the feedback they have received and be given further feedback on the success, or otherwise, of what they are working to improve will help to ensure that the feedback is used.

Make your suggestions only when the learner has exhausted their own. Beware, many people react negatively to or resist advice and it is important that they retain responsibility and control.

Reflect on the last time you gave somebody feedback on how they were doing in their job. How many of the above points did you use ?

Did the feedback motivate the person and lead to better performance?

What can you learn from that experience?

In relation to the feedback that you receive from your own manager, what can you learn about giving feedback to others?

What will your priorities be the next time you have to give feedback to somebody you are coaching?

Summary

In this section we have looked at the five-stage coaching process and the coaching skills that you will need to carry it through. The next step is to put these into practice.

Making it work – applying and reviewing coaching skills

It is now time to begin to apply your awareness of the process and skills of coaching. You will need to use the coaching skills that you have been studying to take a learner through the stages of the coaching process with which you are also familiar.

Recall the coaching process:

- Stage 1 – Identify the need and the opportunity.
- Stage 2 – Agree the goals and objectives.
- Stage 3 – Agree the learning steps.
- Stage 4 – Review.
- Stage 5 – Build on and restart.

And recall the coaching skills:

- cultivating a positive relationship
- creating a learning climate
- questioning
- reinforcing
- giving constructive feedback.

The skills will be applied at each stage of the process to guide the learner through it, while leaving them with the responsibility for seeing things through and making things happen.

What follows is a step-by-step approach to the process that will be useful at this point in giving you an opportunity to see how the stages and skills apply to a real coaching task. The following material examines the five steps of the coaching process and at the end of each step you, as coach, are asked to review what you have learned from each stage.

You will, of course, need a learner, someone prepared to undertake a learning assignment with you as coach. Stage 1 of the process will ask you to start by finding someone keen to progress!

There is no guidance given as to the time required for each stage of the coaching process, as each circumstance will be unique and situations will differ enormously. What is required is to apply the process in a way and at a pace that allows learning to happen at a momentum that suits the learner, the coach and the work situation. It will also be very helpful for the learner to keep their own development planner or notebook to record learning, list plans or simply make notes of useful points.

The coaching process in action

Stage 1 – Identify the need and the opportunity

Remembering that coaching is a natural part of the role of manager, or indeed the natural role of anyone involved in introducing a new member of staff to the tasks required of them or helping a person cover for somebody else's absence, contemplate the situation in your workplace and, having decided who you can work with as coach to help them progress in their work performance or expertise, make a note of the need and opportunity that you have identified.

The person who will benefit from coaching:

____

____

The expertise required:

____

____

The benefits apparent for that person:

____

____

The benefits apparent for me as manager:

____

____

The benefits apparent for the organization:

____

____

This is how I will introduce the opportunity in order to gain the agreement of the learner:

____

____

Bear in mind that the main task at this stage is to motivate the learner. Show them the benefits and assure them of your support. Remember also that people need to feel valued and respected. They need to have their qualities and their potential recognized and not to feel criticized or threatened. Some key questions might be:

- Where do you see yourself progressing to next in your job?
- What would help you make the progress you want?
- What do you need to learn next to build on what you have already achieved?

Make a note of examples of questions that might get the learner to recognize what they might learn to help them progress.

Having identified the need and the opportunity, you should now get the agreement of the learner to work with you through the rest of the process.

Self-review of Stage 1

Make your own notes of your learning after you have completed this stage.

My learning has been:

What, if anything, will I do differently at Stage 1 of any future coaching assignment?

Stage 2 – Agree the goals and objectives

The three key words are 'agree', 'goals' and 'objectives'. Remember that motivation is best promoted by the learner 'owning' the responsibility for their own development. You, as the coach and the manager, will have your views on what is best for the learner, but the skill comes in convincing them, getting them to recognize and accept their development needs. Therefore, this stage is very much about the coach and learner agreeing goals and objectives.

Goals are the overall results that you are seeking through the coaching process. For example, 'The goal is…

- …that you become proficient in the use of the EPOS system'
- …that you can carry out a stock check independently'
- …that you can be acting manager of the department in my absence' and so on.

Overall goals are reached by achieving intermediate objectives. For example, if the goal is 'proficiency in the use of the EPOS system', then intermediate objectives might be:

- 'To understand the purpose and value of EPOS'
- 'To be able to carry out a till reconciliation'
- 'To know which tender types are acceptable'
- 'To know our product codes' and so on.

Think through the coaching assignment on which you have embarked.

The overall goals of this coaching assignment as I see them as coach are:

___

___

The objectives that I believe will provide the stepping stones to achieving those goals are:

Now discuss these with the learner. Listen to their views and between you agree the goals and objectives for the coaching assignment and record them.

Agreed goals:

Agreed objectives:

Ensure that the learner makes a record of these goals and objectives in their personal development planner. The task is to show confidence in the learner's ability and potential. Recognize their current and past achievements while challenging them to make further progress. Get them to 'visualize' themselves with the competences that you wish them to develop. Visualization, picturing ourselves being successful, is a very valuable aid to learning. Valuable questions might be:

- What is it that you want to achieve?
- What are the building blocks to getting there?
- What will it feel like to be able to do that?

Make a note of examples of questions that you could use to get the learner to recognize what their goals and objectives might be.

Don't be afraid to offer suggestions in order to furnish the learner with things to think through.

Self-review of Stage 2

Make your own notes of your learning after you have completed this stage.

My learning has been:

What, if anything, will I do differently at Stage 2 of any future coaching assignment?

Stage 3 – Agree the learning steps

You now have to formulate with the learner the active steps needed to achieve the goals and objectives that you have agreed. The work you have done during Stage 2 should lead naturally into this. Each intermediate objective is likely to require a method for achieving it. Let's continue with the EPOS example. If the goal is 'proficiency in the use of the EPOS system', then the intermediate objectives you might have identified would be:

- 'To understand the purpose and value of EPOS'
- 'To be able to carry out a till reconciliation'
- 'To know which tender types are acceptable'
- 'To know our product codes' and so on.

The learning steps might then be:

- For objective 1 – 'A 20-minute briefing and demonstration from the shop manager'
- For objective 2 – 'Over the next three days, work with a senior assistant as till reconciliations are carried out'
- For objective 3 – 'Work through part 3 of the accounts department training pack' and so on.

Notice that you are helping to design the assignment as well as 'overseeing' it, and helping the learner review progress in it. You do not have to be part of every learning step, although you may well choose to be. Keep in mind the discussion about how adults learn, the importance of creating a learning environment, supporting and challenging, starting where the learner is, different learning styles and designing assignments that are varied, well sequenced, progressive and set at the right pace. Remember in particular to plan for the learner to use what they are learning. Without practice and application there will be no long-term learning!

Make a note of the learning steps you agree with the learner and the timescale to which you will work, including dates by which each step should be accomplished.

Make sure that the learner logs these dates in their diary.

Self-review of Stage 3

Make your own notes of your learning after you have completed this stage.

My learning has been:

What, if anything, will I do differently at Stage 3 of any future coaching assignment?

Stage 4 – Review

At regular intervals during the learning assignment and progression through the learning steps, it will be vital to help the learner review their progress and their learning. Reviewing is important because:

- it consolidates the learning for the learner
- it maintains a sense of progress and momentum
- it allows you or the learner to check out whether there are any problems or a need to revise plans
- it allows you to provide recognition for what the learner is achieving and motivate them to continue their progress.

Write down any questions that you believe will be valuable in such a session and then consider the suggestions that follow.

Suggestions:

- How are you progressing?
- What have you learned so far? Tell me about that.
- What are you learning about yourself through this assignment?
- What have you found most satisfying?
- Would you do anything differently if you had to do that again?
- Is there anything that you would like more help with?
- How are you using what you have learned?

Be conscious of the importance of constructive feedback. Ensure that you are in a position to give the learner feedback on their performance as they progress through the assignment, and especially remember the importance of recognizing achievement!

Planning for reviews

Use your diary to log key dates and times for reviewing learning.

Timing of reviews:

___

___

Place of reviews:

___

___

How I will conduct the review sessions:

___

___

After your review sessions you can carry out your self-review.

Self-review of Stage 4

Make your own notes of your learning as you conduct your review sessions.

My learning has been:

What, if anything, will I do differently at future reviews?

Stage 5 – Build on and restart

It is important for both the learner and the coach to see any learning assignment as just another step in a process of continuous development. Development is continuous both for the learner and the coach, but it is valuable to address the overall goal of life-long learning in a series of learning steps. Rounding off and completing an assignment is therefore an important part of that process. Stage 5 of the coaching process is a final review session. It establishes:

- what has been learned and achieved
- how that will be applied
- what was learned from the experience
- how that will be useful in the future
- what feedback the coach can give the learner
- what feedback the learner can give the coach
- what comes next in terms of development.

That could represent the structure of the session. If you, as a coach, lead the learner through that series of questions, then there is likely to be a sense of completion leading to thoughts about the future.

Remember the key skills. Communicate your appreciation and regard for what the learner has achieved. Make them do the thinking by asking open questions and by offering your version of the answers to support theirs:

- What would you say that you have achieved?
- What are you particularly pleased about and what have been the highlights?
- How could I have been more helpful?
- What will you do with what you have achieved?
- What next?

On the basis of this session, you and the learner can contemplate your next assignment, even if it is not one you will work on together.

Planning the final review session

Time and date of session:

____

____

Place of session:

____

____

My thoughts about how I will conduct it:

____

____

Keep a record of this in your diary or organizer.

Self-review of Stage 5

Make your own notes of your learning after you have completed this stage.

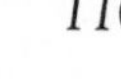

My learning has been:

What, if anything, will I do differently at Stage 5 of any future coaching assignment?

Summary – a final check

Work through the checklist in Table 3.4 of some of the qualities of successful coaches. Ask yourself how true the statements are of you to give you a sense of where your strengths are and what you might focus on in your own development.

How did you do? If you have scored highly in the 'Always true of me' column, then you can be well pleased with your natural coaching ability. Wherever you have ticked one of the other columns, you will have clues about the areas to work on to become even better. You can then review the relevant sections of this chapter to assist in your development.

Congratulations on working through this chapter on coaching. We hope that it has contributed to your learning, but be mindful of the fact that you will never stop learning or developing as a coach. This experience is only a step towards ever-increasing competence in supporting the development of those you work and live with. Any learning materials are only as good as the learner and coach who use them; your skills and talents, your time and your commitment to life-long learning are the biggest gifts you can give to any learner.

In the meantime, don't forget – you don't have to be ill to get better!

Table 3.4 *Coaching qualities checklist*

Statement – successful coaches:	Always true of me	Sometimes true of me	Never true of me
1 Promote participation and involvement, are not directive			
2 Start 'where people are', not where they 'ought to be'			
3 Are patient and tolerant, seen as 'good people'			
4 Are seen as keen on developing themselves; practise what they preach			
5 Are optimistic, encouraging, focus on solutions not problems			
6 Are good communicators			
7 Support and challenge			
8 Look for feedback and take notice of it			
9 Plan things well and prepare thoroughly			
10 Believe a great deal in what they do and are credible people			
11 Trust and show confidence in people			
12 Delegate – not just work or tasks they don't like			
13 Let people get on with things; don't interfere or take over			
14 Are available when guidance is needed			
15 Give constructive feedback regularly			
16 Are good listeners			
17 Show enthusiasm for others' learning			
18 Give other people time and space			
19 Give time to coaching on a regular basis			
20 Take the initiative to encourage learning assignments			

INDEX

70/30 rule in staff development 24–6, 29, 51

achievement (as a job pay-off) 13
action plans 48, 65
alternatives (suggestion of) 45
appraisal of staff 18–20
 see also performance reviews
assumptions 9, 17, 18
 mistakes in 16
attitudes 16, 27, 32

behaviour 4, 8, 9, 16, 22, 33, 44, 45, 47, 48, 51, 62–3
beliefs 27, 51
 see also values
body language 44
boredom 76, 84

career patterns 51–6
 choice 52
challenging questions 94–5
change 9, 20, 23, 46
 in career plans 54, 55, 56
choice 46
 in career patterns 52, 54
coaching 5, 17–18, 67–111
 benefits 71–4, 90, 100
 defined 67–8
 need for 78, 79, 99, 100–2
 objectives 80–1, 82, 92, 99, 102, 103, 104–5
 obstacles 74–7, 91
commitment 23, 39, 57, 67, 110
communication 24, 37, 39, 93, 111
 in staff appraisal 18
competences 1, 2, 4, 5, 6, 16, 32–4, 68, 72–3, 92, 103, 110
 profiles of 32–4
 see also skills
competition 1, 23
conclusions 62, 83
confidence 44, 70, 72, 76, 86, 111
conflict 27
constructive feedback 40, 44–6, 95–8, 99, 107, 111
 see also feedback
counselling 4, 5, 20–21
creativity 52, 57, 85
criticism 45, 62, 69, 70
cultural constraints in feedback 46
customer demands/requirements 23
customisation of products/services 23
cyclical career patterns 53, 54

decision making 20, 27
 defined 5–8
 effectiveness 8–10
 nature of 26, 27–8
 needs (personal) 35
 preventive 6–7
 self-responsibility 24–5
delegation 74, 75, 79, 111
development of staff 1–22
 70/30 rule in staff development 24–6, 29, 51
 nature of 27–31
 see also development reviews

development plans 40–41, 66
 see also development reviews
development reviews 23–66
 benefits 36
 preparations for 41–8, 58–9
 value of 35–6

education 23
efficiency 37
empowerment 28, 44
encouragement 45, 70, 95
enthusiast learning style 83, 84, 85
environment for learning 88–9, 93–4
errors *see* mistakes
evaluation in staff appraisal 18, 19
expectations 47
 of managers 9
expertise 76
 see also skills
extrinsic motivators for learning 87, 88
eye contact *see* body language

feedback 24, 26, 36, 38, 40, 43, 44–6, 48, 62–3, 92, 93, 95–8, 99, 111
 cultural constraints 46
 timing of 97
 see also constructive feedback

goals 10, 26, 36, 37, 38, 39–40, 42, 54, 56, 59, 61, 63, 64–5, 84
 agreeing 80–81, 102–5
 conflicting 64
 in coaching 78, 80–81, 97

'happy workers' 10
horizontal career patterns 52, 53, 54

ideas 45, 83, 84, 85, 93
imaginative learning style 84, 85
impatience 44
inconsistencies 44
information 4, 36, 38, 46, 57, 96
 delivering 17
 overload 17
interpersonal relationships (as a job pay-off) 13, 15
intrinsic motivators for learning 87, 88
intuition 7, 8

job descriptions 1–2
job rotation 38
job satisfaction 2, 5, 49, 52, 72, 73, 87
 defined 10–15
job security 29, 76
jobs (suitability for) 1
judgement 19, 44
 mistakes in 16

knowledge 23, 27, 32, 42, 61, 79
 see also skills

learning 23, 24, 25, 27, 28, 29, 30, 34, 35, 39, 41, 57, 60, 61, 69, 70–71, 99, 101, 104–11
 culture of 38
 environment for 88–9, 93–4
 helps/hindrances 86–9
 in coaching 78, 81–9

motivation for 87–8, 102
participation 88
reinforcement 95
styles of 31–2, 83-6, 90
see also coaching
learning curve 89
listening skills 20, 43, 44, 111
logical learning style 83, 84

measurement in staff appraisal 18
mentoring 4
mistakes 16, 45
misunderstandings 62
morale 7, 9, 10
motivation 10, 22, 24, 32, 53, 70–71, 80, 95, 98, 101, 102
for learning 87–8, 102
multi-skilling 29

nature of supervision (as a job pay-off) 13, 15
need for coaching 78, 79, 99, 100–2
negative feedback 45, 47–8
note taking 99, 103, 105

objectives *see* goals
observational skills 16–17, 22
open questions 94, 109
open thinking 44
opinions 27
see also values
opportunity for advancement (as a job pay-off) 13, 14

participation in learning 88
pay-offs (as motivators) 11–15, 21, 71
performance management *see* appraisal of staff
performance reviews 37–8, 39–40, 42
see also development reviews
personal development 1–22
see also development reviews
planning 38, 39, 40, 43, 84, 85, 111
policy/administration of employers (as a job pay-off) 13, 14
positive feedback *see* constructive feedback
practical learning style 84, 85
praise *see* encouragement
problem solving 2, 4, 27, 74, 83
professional development *see* development reviews
profitability 9, 37
project work 38
promotion 44, 52, 53, 64, 70, 75, 76, 87

qualifications 6
quality 23, 37
questioning skills 94–5
questions 44, 62, 83, 84, 99, 106
challenging questions 94–5

reactions *see* feedback
recognition 30, 87, 95, 107
as a job pay-off 13
recruitment of staff 2–4, 32–4, 38
reinforcement of learning 95

relationships 13, 15, 37, 38, 47–8, 63, 75, 76, 92, 95, 99
remedial training 5, 6
respect 2, 76, 96
feeling of 93, 101
responsibility 38, 46, 64, 74, 91
  as a job pay-off 13, 14
  for self-development 51–6
  shared 41
retention of staff 38
risk 75

salary 64
  as a job pay-off 13, 15
secondments 38, 79
self-awareness 51–6, 63
self-development 49–66
  barriers 28–31
self-esteem 72, 73, 87
skills 2–4, 16, 21, 35, 23, 27, 29, 32, 39, 44, 53, 56, 57, 60, 68, 69, 71, 73, 76, 99, 109, 110
  development 73
  for coaching 78, 91–8, 110, 111
  stages of 78–82
  see also listening skills; observational skills; questioning skills
speed to market 23
staff development 1–22
  70/30 rule in staff development 24–6, 29, 51
  nature of 27–31
  see also coaching; development reviews
staff retention 38
strengths 37, 38
supervision 13, 15
supportive environment for learning 88–9

training 23
  costs 9
  needs 37
  see also staff development
training courses 5, 27

understanding 17, 39, 41, 44, 62, 97
  mistakes in 16
  see also misunderstanding

valued (feeling of) 93, 101
values 7, 8, 27, 32, 39, 46, 58, 60
vertical career patterns 52–3, 54
volatility in customer demands/requirements 23

waste 73
weaknesses 37, 38
work experience 38
work performance (as a job pay-off) 13–14
working conditions (as a job pay-off) 13, 15
workload 75